CONTENTS

1. "Call no man father"?
2. Statue Worship?
3. Constantine and Paganism?
4. Mass a Sacrifice?
5. Baptism: Merely Symbolic?
6. Why Infant Baptism?
7. Saved by Faith Alone?
8. Insufficiency of Redemption?
9. Assurance of Salvation?
10. Tradition Condemned?
11. Changing Doctrines?
12. Why are Priests Celibate?
13. Does Denomination Matter?
14. Which Church Did Jesus Found?

DIOCESE OF GALLUP

711 SOUTH PUERCO DRIVE

P. O. Box 1338 • Gallup, New Mexico 87305 • Telephone (505) 863-4406

February 21, 1994

Mr. Jim Burnham, Pres.
San Juan Catholic Seminars
PO Box 5253
Farmington, NM 87499-5253

Dear Mr. Burnham:

I am happy to send this letter of endorsement for your **"Beginnin** **Apologetics: How to Explain and Defend the Catholic Faith."** I have re the text carefully and found that it is well written and doctrinally sou

As I indicated to you in my letter of December 24, 1993 I believe booklet will serve a good purpose in providing a tool for our Catholic p to explain and defend our faith against those who are antagonistic or tr to do us harm. By the end of Spring we should finally be receiving the h Edition of the **New Universal Catechism.** Because of its limited scope, **B g** **ing** **Apologetics** should be seen <u>within the broader teaching context of the Cate ism</u> <u>and I believe it can serve as a good local supplement to the Catechism.</u>

In closing, I would ask that you refer to the letter of Father Lawrence O'Keefe, my judicial vicar dated December 23, 1993. In this letter to you he suggests you send me the pertinent documentation relating to the San Juan Catholic Seminars so that I can consider giving official Episcopal approval of this organization.

Jim, thank you for all that you do. May the Lord continue to bless all your efforts in a special way.

Fraternally in Christ,

+ ʼ

Most Rev. Donald E. Pelotte, SSS, Ph.D.
Bishop of Gallup

INTRODUCTION

On January 24, 1999, Pope John Paul II isssued a "call to arms" for Catholics to aggressivly confront the challenge of Protestant evangelism. Addressing more than a million people in Mexico City, the Holy Father urged Catholics to ignore the seductions of "fallacious and novel ideologies" and to spread the word of the Church. *"Don't fail to respond to the Master who calls. Follow him to become, like the apostles, fishers of men. Make Christ's word reach those who still don't know him. Have the courage to bear witness to the gospel on the streets and in the town squares, in the valleys and mountains of this nation!"*

Vatican II in its *DECREE ON THE APOSTOLATE OF THE LAITY* said: *"This sacred Synod earnestly exhorts* **laymen**, *each according to his natural gifts and learning,* **to be more diligent in doing their part to explain and defend Christian principles** (no. 6).

The Catholic Church today is being challenged vigorously by non-Catholic evangelizers. Unfortunately, many Catholics feel ill-prepared to defend their faith in the face of these attacks.

San Juan Catholic Seminars is an organization of lay Catholics devoted to **explaining and defending Catholic doctrine**. Our purpose is to strengthen Catholics in their faith by helping them to charitably defend the most commonly challenged Catholic beliefs. We are also commited to resolving doctrinal divisions among Christians by inviting fallen-away Catholics and non-Catholics to consider **the biblical basis for Catholic beliefs**.

We hope this booklet will give Catholics the basic tools to effectively answer the challenges of the many religious groups that come knocking on our doors and to correct some of the misconceptions non-Catholics have about the Catholic Church and its teachings.

We have several other booklets and materials available on apologetics. Please take a look at our mini-catalog at the end of this booklet. We offer bulk discounts so that you can easily strengthen your family and friends. For more information, or for bookstore pricing, please contact us at:

San Juan Catholic Seminars
P. O. Box 5253
Farmington, NM 87499-5253

FAX: (505) 327-9554
Phone: (505) 327-5343

A BEGINNER'S GUIDE TO APOLOGETICS

"Apologetics" simply means **giving a reasoned explanation for your faith**. A Catholic apologist charitably explains and defends Catholic doctrine using Scripture, history, and common sense.

Apologetics fulfills the command of St. Peter: "*Always be ready to give an explanation to anyone who asks you for a reason for your hope, but do it with gentleness and reverence...*" (1 Pet 3:15-16). A beginning apologist must remember the following points:

1. **Holiness**. Base apologetics on the love of God and His Truth. An apologist who is not concerned with personal holiness will not be very effective.

2. **Charity**. Remember that you are a missionary, not a debater. Your goal is to explain and evangelize, not to win arguments. You must have charity at all times, even in the most heated discussions.

3. **Unity**. Begin by stressing that we agree with other Christians on many important points. Acknowledge the sincerity and zeal of our separated brothers in Christ.

4. **Study**. Be prepared to study at least 30 minutes three times per week. Read the Bible 20 minutes, and use the other 10 minutes to read a good Catholic catechism. In your study of the Bible, concentrate on the New Testament. Be sure to highlight important passages and use the cross-references and footnotes.

5. **Equal time**. Do not allow the non-Catholic evangelizer to take up all the time or ask all the questions. Divide the time equally and ask him a few challenging questions of your own.

6. **Focus**. Insist on staying on the main issues during the discussion. Don't let the other person ask a dozen different questions and expect you to answer them all in ten minutes. Explain the need to stay focused and to allow plenty of time for answers. The chief concern is to shed light on the truth, not to make cheap debating points.

7. **Topics**. Do not feel obligated to stick with the subjects non-Catholics bring up—especially if you're not familiar with them. Insist on talking about the Eucharist at the start of your discussion because it is so important and because it divides Catholics from virtually all Protestants. (See p. 7.)

8. **Interpretation**. Do not accept the Protestant interpretation of a verse when it contradicts Catholic doctrine. Read it yourself *in context* and show how the verse can be interpreted to support the Catholic position. Protestants often distort Bible verses to fit their denominational teaching.

9. **Canon of the Bible**. Show how the Bible was put together by the Catholic Church. Stress the fact that Christianity was around for 350 years before the canon of the New Testament was determined. (See p. 10.)

10. **Historical perspective**. Have non-Catholics stand back and look at Church history. Get them to see that many Protestant beliefs were *unheard of* for 1500 years after Christ established His Church. Never end a discussion without stressing the fact that *all* the early Church Fathers were

Catholic in their beliefs. Know a few of the early Church Fathers well: especially St. Ignatius of Antioch, St. Justin Martyr, and St. Irenaeus. (See p. 9.)

11. **Knowledge**. Explain Catholic beliefs clearly. This is your primary task. Keep a good catechism handy for this purpose. Don't try to defend a doctrine that you don't understand. If you don't know the answer to a question, honestly admit it and tell them you will get back to them later on the subject after you have done some study.

12. **Tempers**. Begin and end the discussion with *prayer*. Keep control of your temper. Apologize if you lose it. Calmly end the discussion if the other person becomes abusive in his approach. Insist that they refrain from abusive attacks on Our Lady and the Eucharist. Ask them simply to state where they disagree and why.

13. **Expertise**. Don't be afraid if you are not an expert in Catholic doctrine. You don't have to be; just give them what you know. If you can make just one good point, or correct just one misunderstanding, you have already accomplished a lot. Besides, the very fact that a non-Catholic met a Catholic who is polite, knowledgeable about the Bible, and concerned about saving souls will itself leave a good impression of the Catholic Church.

14. **Caution**. Be careful whom you let into your home! Being an apologist doesn't mean throwing away common sense when it comes to trusting strangers.

PRACTICAL POINTS ON BIBLE READING

1. Get a Bible that is **comfortable to read**. Large print is generally best for most people. Those who have difficulty reading should get giant print.

2. Choose a good **translation** of the Bible. The three versions approved for liturgical use in this country are the 1970 *NEW AMERICAN BIBLE* (NAB), the *JERUSALEM BIBLE*, and the *REVISED STANDARD VERSION CATHOLIC EDITION* (RSVCE). We recommend the NAB, with the RSVCE as a back-up.[1]

3. Use Bible **tabs** and a **soft cover** Bible. This allows you to find verses quickly. Remember that time is critical in apologetics. You don't want to spend *your* 15 minutes looking up a Bible passage. Practice, and become proficient at quickly finding verses.

4. Pick a Bible that has **newspaper-type columns**. These are easier to read, and make passages easier to identify. Choose a Bible that has the cross-references and footnotes on the same page as this saves time. It is also helpful if your Bible has a dictionary and doctrinal index at the end.

5. Avoid arguments over **translations**. You can almost always defend the Catholic position from any translation. (There are exceptions: for example, the Jehovah's Witnesses have a very mangled translation called the *NEW WORLD TRANSLATION*, which you should avoid.)

6. Stay away from arguments over the **Greek or Hebrew meanings** of the words.[2] Splitting hairs over the precise meaning of the original Greek and Hebrew words is often used as a diversionary tactic by Fundamentalists. Emphasize that the best Greek and Hebrew scholars were involved in giving us the standard modern versions and that you are willing to use any of these. Stress that *doctrinal differences are almost never due to bad translations*. We have excellent translations in our time, both Catholic and Protestant. The differences arise over what the words, *accurately translated*, **mean**. What we need are good cross-references, Church history, and reason.

7. Underline or **highlight verses** and **makes notes** in your Bible. Your study Bible is not a decoration or family heirloom.

8. Don't try to memorize exact chapter and verse, except for a few very critical passages. **Memorize the chapter or chapters**. If you have highlighted well, the doctrinally important verse will stand out immediately when you get within a chapter or two of it.

---

[1] Unless noted, we have used the *NEW AMERICAN BIBLE*, 1970, 1986, throughout this booklet.

[2] Obviously, a knowledge of Greek and Hebrew can be very useful for studying the Bible and refuting misinterpretations. However, you can be an effective apologist without knowing any biblical languages.

THE EUCHARIST

Catholics believe that the Eucharist is the *literal* body and blood of Christ. Virtually all of the more than 25,000 different Protestant denominations believe Christ is only present *symbolically* in the Eucharist.

Because the Eucharist is such an important doctrine, and because it divides us from nearly all Protestants, a Catholic must insist on discussing the Eucharist in any apologetic dialogue, and he must be prepared to discuss it *well.*

In order to defend the biblical basis for the **Real Presence of Christ in the Eucharist**, read and study the following passages:

all of **John 6**	**Mt 26:26-28**
Mk 14:22-24	**Lk 22:17-20**
1 Cor 10:14-17	**Lk 24:30-35**
1 Cor 11:23-29	

Be able to "walk" a non-Catholic step by step through **John 6**. Begin by reading **Jn 4:31-34** and **Mt 16:5-12**, which describe Jesus speaking about food in a *symbolic* or figurative way. The disciples interpret Him to mean real food. Note how Jesus shows them in plain, unmistakable language that He is only speaking *figuratively.*

Compare this with **Jn 6:51**. Jesus says we must eat His flesh in order to have life. In **Jn 6:52**, the Jews *interpret Him literally.* Jesus then repeats again and again (verses **53-56**)—in the clearest possible language—that we must eat His flesh and drink His blood in order to have eternal life. Take special note of verse **55**: *"my flesh is true food and my blood is true drink"*—**this is not the language of symbolism.**

Protestants often cite John 6:35: *"I am the bread of life; whoever **comes** to me will never hunger; whoever **believes** in me will never thirst."* They claim that when Jesus calls Himself the "bread of life" He is simply saying that if we believe in Him, He will nourish us spiritually, just as bread nourishes us physically. Protestants claim that we "eat" and "drink" Jesus, our spiritual food, by **coming** to and **believing** in Him.

However, we must read the rest of this Eucharistic discourse, especially verses 48-58, where Jesus tells us exactly what He means by calling Himself "bread." The bread Jesus is speaking of is not merely a symbol for spiritual nourishment. Jesus tells us plainly that the bread is **His own flesh** (verse **51**), which we must eat in order to have eternal life. When Jesus explains that the bread of life is literally His flesh, we must accept His clear words.

Many Protestants claim that, in **John 6:60-70**, Jesus explains that He was only speaking symbolically in the previous verses. They focus on verse **63**, *"It is the spirit that gives life, while the flesh is of no avail. The words I have spoken to you are spirit and life."* Be prepared to deal with this objection as follows:

(a) Jesus' Eucharistic talk *ends* with verse **58** (see verse **59**). The dialogue of verses **60-70** occurs *later* and deals with **faith**, not the Eucharist.

(b) The word "spirit" is nowhere used in the Bible to mean "symbolic." The spiritual is just as real as the material.

(c) In verse **63**, Jesus is contrasting the natural or carnal man (*"the flesh"*) with the spiritual or faith-filled man. Read **1 Cor 2:14-3:4** for a good explanation of what Jesus means by "*the flesh*." Note that Jesus says "*my flesh*" when discussing the Eucharist. He says "*the flesh*" when referring to the carnal man who will not believe anything beyond his senses and reason. No Christian believes that Jesus' flesh is "of no avail," for His flesh was the means of our redemption.

(d) Note that the unbelieving disciples leave Jesus *after* verse 63—**they would not have left at this point if Jesus had assured them that He was only speaking symbolically**. This is the only time recorded in the New Testament that any of Jesus' disciples left Him because they found a doctrine of His too hard to accept. Of the twelve Apostles, apparently only Judas rejected the Eucharist (Jn 6:70-71).

Now read the other Eucharistic Bible passages. Again and again the biblical language indicates the Real Presence of Christ in the Eucharist. Note the strong language of St. Paul in **1 Cor 11:27**, "*whoever eats the bread or drinks the cup of the Lord unworthily **sins against the body and blood of the Lord**.*"

In the Aramaic language that Our Lord spoke, to symbolically "eat the flesh" or "drink the blood" of someone meant to persecute and assault him. See Ps 27:2; Isaiah 9:18-20; Isaiah 49:26; Micah 3:3; 2 Sam 23:15-17; and Rev 17:6, 16. Thus, if Jesus were only speaking *symbolically* about eating His flesh and drinking His blood, as the Protestants say, then what He really meant was "**whoever persecutes and assaults me will have eternal life.**" This, of course, makes nonsense of the passage!

Consider Christ's use of bread and wine at the Last Supper. Bread and wine are not normal or natural symbols of flesh and blood. Yet in all four Last Supper accounts (Mt 26:26-28; Mk 14:22-24; Lk 22:17-20; 1 Cor 11:23-25) Jesus tells us plainly that "this IS my body" and " this IS my blood." Never is there a hint that He is speaking symbolically. Either the symbols would have been **clearly** explained if He were speaking symbolically (which is not the case) or Jesus spoke **literally** (which is the case!).

Occasionally, a non-Catholic will insist that we Catholics, because of our belief about the Eucharist, *engage in cannibalism and violate the biblical prohibition on the drinking of blood*. It was exactly this misunderstanding that led the unbelieving Jews and disciples in John 6 to reject Jesus when He spoke about the need to eat His body and drink His blood. The believing disciples were rewarded for their faith at the Last Supper. Jesus revealed to them that they would receive His body and blood in the *sacrament* of the Holy Eucharist, not in the bloody, cannibalistic way the unbelievers had imagined.

All the early Church Fathers believed in the Real Presence (see Appendix 1, page 9). Until the Reformation, all Christianity accepted the Real Presence of Christ in the Eucharist. Even Martin Luther affirmed the doctrine.[3] Note that all the Churches that

---

3 "*Who*, but the devil, hath granted such a license of wresting the words of the holy Scripture? Who ever read in the Scriptures, that *my body* is the same as the *sign of my body*? or, that *is* is the same as *it signifies*? What language in the world ever spoke so? It is only then the *devil*, that imposeth upon us by these fanatical men.... Not one of the Fathers, though so numerous, ever spoke as the Sacramentarians: not one of them ever said, *It is only bread and wine*; or, *the body and blood of*

broke away *before* the Reformation (Orthodox, Coptic, Armenian) still believe in the Real Presence.

Finally, mention some of the great Eucharistic miracles that God has given us to confirm the Real Presence of Christ in the Eucharist. Joan Cruz's *EUCHARISTIC MIRACLES*[4] is an excellent resource for this purpose. Many of these miracles have been *scientifically verified*.

Appendix 1: Early Church Fathers on the Eucharist

St. Ignatius of Antioch, a disciple and contemporary of the Apostle John, wrote (around 110 A.D.) concerning certain heretics: "*They abstain from the Eucharist and from prayer, because they do not confess that **the Eucharist is the Flesh of our Savior Jesus Christ**, Flesh which suffered for our sins and which the Father, in His goodness, raised up again.*"[5]

In another letter St. Ignatius writes, "*I desire the Bread of God, which is the **Flesh of Jesus Christ** ... and for drink I desire **His Blood**, which is love incorruptible.*"[6]

Christ is not there present. Surely it is not *credible*, nor *possible*, since they often speak, and repeat their sentiments, that they should never (if they thought so) not so much as once, say, or let slip these words: *It is bread only*; or *the body of Christ is not there*, especially it being of great importance, that men should not be deceived. Certainly in so many Fathers, and in so many writings, the *negative* might at least be found *in one of them*, had they *thought the body and blood of Christ were* not really present: but they are all of them unanimous." (*LUTHER'S COLLECTED WORKS*, Wittenburg Edition, no. 7, p. 391).

[4] (Rockford, Ill.: TAN Books, 1988).
[5] *LETTER TO THE SMYRNAEANS* 6, 2; William A. Jurgens, *THE FAITH OF THE EARLY FATHERS* (Collegeville, Minn.: Liturgical Press, 1970), Vol. 1, p. 25, #64.
[6] *LETTER TO THE ROMANS* 7, 3; Jurgens, p. 22, #54a.

St. Justin Martyr wrote in his apology to the emperor at Rome (around 150 A.D.): "*We call this food Eucharist; and no one else is permitted to partake of it, except one who believes our teaching to be true.... For not as common bread nor common drink do we receive these; but since Jesus Christ our Savior was made incarnate by the word of God and had both flesh and blood for our salvation, so too, as we have been taught, the food which has been made into the Eucharist by the Eucharistic prayer set down by Him, and by the change of which our blood and flesh is nourished, **is both the Flesh and the Blood of that incarnated Jesus**.*"[7]

St. Irenaeus, bishop of Lyons and a pupil of St. Polycarp who had been taught by St. John the Apostle, wrote (around 195 A.D.): "*He [Jesus] has declared the cup, a part of creation, to be **His own Blood**, from which He causes our blood to flow; and the bread, a part of creation, He has established as **His own Body**, from which He gives increase to our bodies.*"[8]

St. Cyril of Jerusalem, in a catechetical lecture given in the middle of the fourth century (350 A.D.), said: "*Do not, therefore, regard the bread and wine as simply that; **for they are**, according to the Master's declaration, **the Body and Blood of Christ**. Even though the senses suggest to you the other, let faith make you firm. Do not judge in this matter by taste, but be fully assured by the faith, not doubting that you have been deemed worthy of **the Body and Blood of Christ**.*"[9]

---

[7] *FIRST APOLOGY*, 66, 20; Jurgens, p. 55, #128.
[8] *AGAINST HERESIES*, 5, 2, 2; Jurgens, p. 99, #249.
[9] *CATECHETICAL LECTURES*: [*MYSTAGOGIC* 4], 22, 6; Jurgens, p. 361, #846.

THE CANON OF THE BIBLE

Thinking Christians realize that if God has revealed Himself to man, we must be able to know *with assurance* where that revelation can be found. Since we are staking our salvation on the truth of God's word, **we need to know exactly and infallibly** *which books* **contain divine truth**. Otherwise we might look to the words of men for the Word of God. Thus we need an authoritative list (canon) of the inspired books of the Bible. "Canon" means a measuring standard. The **canon of Scripture** refers to a standard, or official list of inspired books that make up the Bible.

THE OLD TESTAMENT (OT)

Why do Catholic and Protestant Bibles have a different number of books in the OT?

The Protestant OT is based on the **Palestinian** (or Hebrew) **canon** used by Hebrew-speaking Jews in Palestine. The Catholic OT is based on the **Alexandrian** (or Greek) **canon** used by the Greek-speaking Jews throughout the Mediterranean, including Palestine.

The city of Alexandria in Egypt possessed the greatest library in the ancient world and during the reign of Ptolemy II Philadelphus (285-246 BC), a translation of the entire Hebrew Bible into Greek was begun by 70 or 72 Jewish scholars—according to tradition—six from each of the twelve tribes. From this Alexandrian translation (completed between 250-125 BC) we get the term "Septuagint," Latin for 70 (LXX), the number of translators.

This Greek translation of the OT was very popular because Greek was the common language of the entire Mediterranean world by the time of Christ. Hebrew was a dying language (Jews in Palestine usually spoke Aramaic), and so it is not surprising that **the Septuagint was the translation used by Jesus and the New Testament writers**. In fact, 300 quotations from the OT found in the New Testament are from the Septuagint. Remember also that the entire New Testament was written in **Greek**.

The Septuagint contains 46 books. The Hebrew canon contains only 39. *Why are there seven fewer books in the Hebrew canon?*

The Hebrew canon was established by Jewish rabbis at Jamnia, in Palestine about the year 100 A.D., perhaps in reaction to the Christian Church, which was using the Alexandrian canon. The Jews at Jamnia rejected seven books from the Hebrew canon found in the Septuagint–**Wisdom, Sirach, Judith, Baruch, Tobit, and 1 and 2 Maccabees** (as well as portions of Daniel and Esther)–chiefly on the grounds that *they could not find any Hebrew versions of these books* which the Septuagint supposedly translated into Greek.[10]

The Christian Church continued to use the Septuagint. When the Church officially decided which books comprise the canon of the Bible (Councils of Hippo, 393 A.D., and Carthage, 397 A.D.), **it approved the 46 books of the Alexandrian canon as the canon for the OT**. For sixteen centuries the Alexandrian canon was a matter of

---

10 The Council of Jamnia used four criteria to determine their canon. They accepted only those books which were: (1) writ-

uncontested faith. Each of the seven rejected books is quoted by the early Church Fathers as "Scripture" or as "inspired," **right along with the undisputed books.**[11]

In 1529 Martin Luther proposed the Palestinian canon of 39 books in Hebrew as the OT canon. Luther found justification for removing the seven books from the Bible in the old concerns of St. Jerome and the Council of Jamnia that the Greek books had no Hebrew counterparts. However, research into the Dead Sea Scrolls found at Qumran has *discovered ancient Hebrew copies of some of the disputed books,*[12] making their rejection unsupportable on those grounds.

But here is the real question: *Which OT would you rather use—the OT used by Jesus, the NT writers and the early Church, or the OT used by the Jews who rejected Christ and persecuted Christianity?*

If your Bible includes the seven books, you follow Jesus and the early Church. If your Bible omits the seven books, you follow the non-Christian Jews at Jamnia and Martin Luther—a man who wanted to throw out even **more** books (James, Esther, Revelation), and who deliberately added the word "alone" to Sacred Scripture in his German translation of Romans 3:28.

---

ten in Hebrew; (2) in conformity with the Torah; (3) older than the time of Ezra (c. 400 B.C.); and (4) written in Palestine.

[11] Some of the Fathers include Polycarp, Irenaeus, Clement, and Cyprian. For a collection of patristic quotations from each of the disputed books, see "The Fathers Know Best: Old Testament Canon" in the October 1993 issue of THIS ROCK magazine (Vol. 4, No. 10, pp. 25-27).

[12] *NEW CATHOLIC COMMENTARY ON HOLY SCRIPTURE* (Nashville, Tenn.: Thomas Nelson, 1975), p. 22.

THE NEW TESTAMENT (NT)

The first word of the NT was written about 50 A.D. (1 Thess), the last word between 90-100 A.D. (Rev), for a total of 27 books, all of which are accepted as canonical and inspired by Catholics and Protestants alike. The question is, **who determined the NT canon of inspired books?** The Bible didn't fall from heaven pre-printed, so where did we get it? How do we know we can trust every book?

Various bishops developed lists of inspired books:

Mileto, Bishop of Sardis, c. 175 A.D.
St. Irenaeus, Bishop of Lyons, 185 A.D.
Eusebius, Bishop of Caesarea, c. 325 A.D.

Pope Damasus in 382 A.D., prompted by the Council of Rome, wrote a decree listing the present OT and NT canon of 73 books.

The Council of Hippo (in North Africa) in 393 A.D. approved the present OT and NT canon of 73 books.

The Council of Carthage (in North Africa) in 397 A.D. approved the same OT and NT canon. *This is the council which many Protestants and Evangelicals take as the authority for the NT canon of books.*

Pope St. Innocent I (401-417) in 405 A.D., approved the 73-book canon and **closed the canon of the Bible.**

The canon of the Bible was officially determined in the fourth century by Catholic councils and Catholic popes. Until the canon was decided, there was much debate. Some were of the opinion that certain canonical books, **Hebrews, Jude, Revelation, 2 Peter,** *were not inspired,* while others held that certain noncanonical books, **Shepherd of Hermas, Gospels of Peter and Thomas,** the **letters of Barnabas** and **Clement,** *were inspired.* The formal Church decision settled the matter for the next 1100 years. Not until the Reformation was there any more debate about the contents of the Bible.

Historically, **the Catholic Church used her authority to determine which books belonged to the Bible, and to assure us that everything in the Bible is inspired.** Apart from the Church, we simply have no way of knowing either truth.

Martin Luther himself admits, *"We are obliged to yield many things to the Papists [Catholics]—that they possess the Word of God which we received from them, otherwise we should have known nothing at all about it."*[13] Luther is admitting that Christians owe their Bible to the efforts of the Catholic Church.

Luther's statement supports our argument that **without the decisions of the Church, we would not know which books of the Bible are inspired.** As St. Augustine says, *"I would put no faith in the Gospels unless the authority of the Catholic Church directed me to do so."*[14] St. Augustine recognizes that the only way to determine which books are inspired is to accept the teaching authority of the Catholic Church.

CRUCIAL POINTS

(1) **Historically,** the Bible is a Catholic book. The New Testament was written, copied, and collected by Catholic Christians. **The official canon of the books of the Bible was authoritatively determined by the Catholic Church in the fourth century.** Thus it is *from the Catholic Church* that the Protestants have a Bible at all.

(2) **Logically,** the Church with the authority to determine the infallible Word of God, must have the infallible authority and guidance of the Holy Spirit. As we have seen, apart from the declarations of the Catholic Church, we have absolutely no guarantee that what is in the Bible is the genuine Word of God. *To trust the Bible is to trust the authority of the Church which guarantees the Bible.* **It is contradictory for Protestants to accept the Bible and yet reject the authority of the Catholic Church.**

Logically, Protestants should not quote the Bible at all, for they have no way of determining which books are inspired— unless, of course, they accept the teaching authority of the Catholic Church.

13 *COMMENTARY ON ST. JOHN,* ch. 16.
14 *CONTRA EPISTOLAM MANICHAEI,* 5, 6.

THE BIBLE ALONE?

Almost all Protestants follow the doctrine of **Sola Scriptura**. This doctrine claims that the *Bible alone* is the authority in matters of faith. Fundamentalists will begin by saying: "Let's agree that the Bible is the sole rule of faith." A Catholic must answer with a firm, "*NO!*" **They are really asking you to reject Sacred Tradition and the authority of the Church**.

We must show them that **Christ left a Church to teach, govern, and sanctify in His name until the end of time**. To reject that authority is to reject Christ and His Gospel. We Catholics accept the Bible as an authority in matters of faith because it is God's inspired Word. However, we cannot accept it as the **only** rule of faith for the following reasons.

It goes against the *BIBLE*. Scripture tells us that Christ left a Church with *divine authority to govern* in His name (Mt 16:13-20, 18:18; Lk 10:16). Christ promised that this Church *would last until the end of time* (Mt 16:18, 28:19-20; Jn 14:16). The Bible also tells us that *Sacred Tradition is to be followed alongside Sacred Scripture* (2 Thess 2:15, 3:6).

The doctrine of sola scriptura is not found in Scripture. In fact, the Bible tells us that we need more than just the Bible alone. The Bible confirms that *not everything Jesus said and did is recorded* in Scripture (John 21:25) and that we must also hold fast to *oral tradition, the **preached** Word of God* (1 Cor 11:2; 1 Pet 1:25). In 2 Pet 3:15-16, we are warned that Sacred Scripture can be very difficult to interpret, which strongly implies the need for an authoritative interpreter. Finally, 1 Tim 3:15 reassures us that the Church is "the pillar and foundation of truth."

It goes against *HISTORY*. The history of the Bible attests that it was the Church exercising its Apostolic authority that determined what is and is not Scripture. We need the authority of the Church to tell us what belongs in the Bible (1 Tim 3:15).

It goes against *COMMON SENSE*. Any written document meant to play a crucial role in determining how people live must have a living, continuing authority to guard, guarantee, and officially interpret it. **Otherwise, chaos reigns as everyone interprets the document according to his personal whim**.

For example, the Founding Fathers of this country put together a magnificent document to be authoritative in determining how this country would be governed: the U. S. Constitution. They also established a living, continuing authority to guard, guarantee, and officially interpret the Constitution: the Supreme Court.

The Founding Fathers knew that without a living authority the Constitution would lead to endless divisions as every one acted as his own interpreter. God certainly has more wisdom than the founders of this country. **He would never have left a written document to be the only rule of faith without a living authority to guard and officially interpret it**.

In summary, the splintering of Christianity into over 25,000 denominations is the direct fruit of the Bible-alone doctrine. This idea does not come from God and was unheard of for 1500 years before the Reformation.

APOSTOLIC AUTHORITY PETER AND THE PAPACY

Protestants reject apostolic succession in general and the teaching authority of the bishop of Rome in particular. You should focus on papal authority because it has **strong support in Scripture**, and it can be easily **traced historically**.

SCRIPTURE

In the OT, when God established His Covenant with the nation of Israel, He provided for a **living, continuing authority** in the Mosaic priesthood (see 2 Chr 19:11; Mal 2:7.) This authority did not end when the OT Scripture was written; rather, it continued as the safeguard and authentic interpreter of Sacred Scripture.

When Christ established His Church, the New Israel, He set up a **living, continuing authority to teach, govern, and sanctify in His name**. This living authority is called "Apostolic" because it began with the twelve Apostles and continued with their successors. It was this Apostolic authority that would preserve and authentically interpret the Revelation of Jesus Christ. This same Apostolic authority determined the canon of the Bible, and will preserve the teachings of Jesus Christ in all their fullness, and uncorrupted from error, until the end of time.

Among the twelve Apostles, St. Peter is clearly the head. Know **Matthew 16:13-19** well: "*And so I say to you, you are Peter [Rock], and upon this rock I will build my church, and the gates of the netherworld shall not prevail against it. I will give you the keys to the kingdom of heaven. Whatever you bind on earth shall be bound in heaven; and whatever you loose on earth shall be loosed in heaven.*'"

Jesus changes Simon's name to Peter, which mean "rock."[15] Our Lord says this **rock** will be God's way of preserving the Church from corruption until the end of time. Our Lord knew St. Peter would be dead by 70 A.D. Therefore Christ must have intended the **office of Peter** to last until the end of time. St. Peter is given the "keys to the kingdom of heaven."[16] This is an awesome gift. To nobody else does Christ give this ruling power. Ask non-Catholics to reflect on this unique privilege instead of trying, by verbal acrobatics, to explain away the title "Peter."

---

[15] Many Protestants argue that Jesus is not building His Church on Peter by pointing out that, in the Greek text, the word used for Peter is *Petros*, a masculine noun, while the word used for rock is *petra*, a feminine noun. *Petros* means "small stone," while *petra* means "massive rock." They claim, therefore, that the "massive rock" (*petra*) upon which Christ will build His Church must not refer to Peter the "small stone" (*Petros*) but rather to Peter's profession of faith or to Jesus. However, Jesus spoke Aramaic, which leaves no room for the Greek *Petros/petra* distinction. In Aramaic, the word for rock is *kepha*. What Christ said was, "You are *Kepha* (Rock) and upon this *kepha* (rock) I will build my Church." In Aramaic, the identification of Peter as the rock is clear.

Why does the Greek use two different words for Peter and the rock? Because the Greek word for rock, *petra*, is feminine. It would not be appropriate to give a man a feminine name. So the translator gave *petra* a masculine ending and rendered it *Petros*. Since *petros* was a preexisting word meaning "small stone," some of the original word-play was lost. But no early Church Father, including those who spoke Greek as their mother-tongue, ever saw a distinction between Peter and the rock. They are unanimous in teaching that Peter is the rock on which Christ built His Church.

[16] Jesus is drawing this image of "the keys" from Is 22:19-22. From this context, at least three concepts are included. (1) The keys are a symbol of the **authority** given to the chief official—the Prime Minister—of the Kingdom of David. (2) The Prime Minister is a **father-figure**. Remember, "Pope" comes from the Italian word for "Papa"—father. (3) The office implies dynastic **succession**. The office of Prime Minister continued as long as the Kingdom of David continued. Catholics believe that Christ is the King, and that the Pope is the "Prime Minister" of His heavenly kingdom, the Church. Christ is the Head of the Church; the Pope is His earthly representative.

Ask them why Jesus would give this tremendous authority to St. Peter and **not intend for it to be passed on**. If the early Christians needed an authoritative leader, later Christians would need one even more. After all, many of the early Christians heard the Gospel from Christ Himself and knew the Apostles personally. After all the Apostles died, the Church would have even greater need of the power of the keys when enemies would try to corrupt the teachings of Christ.

Although all the Apostles as a group were given the power to "bind and to loose" in Mt 18:18, St. Peter received this power individually at the time he was given the "keys." Point out that Jesus would not have guaranteed to back up the doctrinal teachings of St. Peter and his successors **unless He was also going to protect them from teaching false doctrine in their official capacities as Shepherds of the Church**.

Also know **Lk 22:31-32** and **John 21:15-17**. In the passage from St. Luke, Jesus prays that Peter's faith would not fail; Peter in turn would strengthen the other disciples. In the passage from St. John, Jesus clearly makes Peter the shepherd of His Church. So St. Peter is the **rock** on which Christ builds His Church. He is given the "**keys of the Kingdom**;" and he is made **shepherd** of Christ's flock: solid biblical evidence that Jesus made St. Peter the first Pope. The popes are Christ's vicars, the visible and earthly heads of Christ's Church while Christ is the invisible and supreme head.

Be familiar with **Acts 15**. This gives an account of the first Church council, the Council of Jerusalem. Called at the request of St. Paul, this council met to decide whether Gentiles had to follow the Law of Moses as well as the Law of Christ. Notice that there was much discussion among the Apostles and presbyters. However, **after Peter spoke, the assembly fell silent**. His statement ended the discussion. This council obviously considered St. Peter's authority final.

Some Fundamentalists claim Acts 15 shows that James, not Peter, was the head of the Church. Since James the Less (not James, the brother of John) gives the concluding remarks at the council of Jerusalem and also recommends some marriage and dietary regulations for the Gentiles, they conclude that James must be the head of the Church.

We must remind Fundamentalists to read the Gospels, where St. Peter is unmistakably presented as a leader among the Apostles, whereas St. James the Less is not.[17] Ask Fundamentalists to read the first twelve chapters of Acts, which describe the early Church in Jerusalem. Every chapter (except 6 and 7, which describe Stephen's martyrdom) shows St. Peter in a leadership position while St. James appears only briefly, and never in a leadership role.[18] In Galatians 1:18-19, we are told that Paul went

---

[17] Peter often spoke for the rest of the Apostles (Mt 19:27; Mk 8:29; Lk 12:41; Jn 6:69). The Apostles are sometimes referred to as "Peter and his companions" (Lk 9:32; Mk 16:7; Acts 2:37). Peter's name always heads the list of the Apostles (Mt 10:1-4; Mk 3:16-19; Lk 6:14-16; Acts 1:13). Finally, Peter's name is mentioned 191 times, which is more than all the rest of the Apostles combined (about 130 times). After Peter, the most frequently mentioned Apostle is John, whose name appears 48 times.

[18] Peter is conspicuously involved in all the Church's important "firsts." Peter led the meeting which elected the first successor to an Apostle (Acts 1:13-26). Peter preached the first sermon at Pentecost (Acts 2:14), and received the first converts (Acts 2:41). Peter performed the first miracle after Pentecost (Acts 3:6-7), inflicted the first punishment upon Ananias and Saphira (Acts 5:1-11), and excommunicated the

to Jerusalem after his conversion specifically to confer with Peter. He stayed with Peter 15 days. In contrast, Paul visited James only briefly during this time.

At the council of Jerusalem in Acts 15, it was St. Peter's statements that settled the serious doctrinal dispute that was the reason for the council. As we saw earlier, St. Peter's statements **silenced** the assembly of presbyters and the Apostles (including St. James).

We know from Church history that St. James was the Bishop of Jerusalem and, as Acts 21:15-25 describes, he was concerned for Jewish Christians in Jerusalem who felt their ancient customs threatened by the great number of Gentile converts. This background explains why St. James made the concluding remarks at the council and asked Gentiles to respect certain Jewish practices. Fundamentalists are grasping at straws when they claim that Acts 15 proves that James, instead of Peter, was the head of the Church.

Fundamentalists will also cite 1 Peter 5:1 to claim that Peter was not the head of the Church. They note that Peter, in addressing some elders (Church leaders), calls himself a **fellow** elder. They therefore conclude that Peter had no more authority than any other elder. But this is just like the President of the United States saying, "My fellow Americans." This would certainly **not** indicate that the President has no more authority than an ordinary citizen.

As an Apostle, St. Peter certainly considers his authority to be greater than that of an ordinary elder. After all, St. Peter goes on to admonish these "fellow elders" (1 Pet 5:2-4) as one having authority over them. In calling them fellow elders, St. Peter is simply acknowledging the obvious: like himself, they are also Church leaders. For Fundamentalists to insist that Peter, as an Apostle, had no greater authority than an ordinary elder, shows how little they appreciate what Scripture says about the great office of Apostle.

Many Fundamentalists quote **Gal 2:11-14** as well, attempting to show that Peter was not infallible[19] and that Paul did not consider him the head of the Church. This position is not supportable. First of all, **if they think Peter was not infallible, why do they accept his two letters as inspired and, therefore, infallible**? We must accept that all the Apostles were infallible. After the Apostles, the popes individually and the bishops as a group in union with the pope, are infallible.

St. Paul correcting St. Peter for weak behavior is no different from St. Catherine of Siena correcting weak popes in the Middle Ages. There was no doctrine involved. St. Peter himself had settled the doctrinal point at the Council of Jerusalem. St. Paul corrected St. Peter for being unwilling to confront the Judaizers from Jerusalem. Remember, St. Paul was among those who fell silent at the Council of Jerusalem once St. Peter spoke.

---

first heretic, Simon the magician (Acts 8:21). Peter is the first Apostle to raise a person from the dead (Acts 9:36-41). Peter first received the revelation to admit Gentiles into the Church (Acts 10:9-16), and commanded that the first Gentile converts be baptized (Acts 10:44-48).

---

[19] "Infallible" means incapable of teaching error in matters of faith and morals. It does not mean impeccable: incapable of committing sin.

HISTORY

Please note that the early Church always accepted the Bishop of Rome as head of the Church. In about 80 A.D., the Church at Corinth deposed its lawful leaders. The fourth bishop of Rome, Pope Clement I, was called to settle the matter even though St. John the Apostle was still alive and much closer to Corinth than was Rome.[20]

St. Irenaeus, who was taught by St. Polycarp (a disciple of St. John the Apostle), stresses that **Christians must be united to the Church of Rome in order to maintain the Apostolic Tradition.** He then lists all the bishops of Rome up to his time.[21] St. Irenaeus presents this teaching as something taken for granted by orthodox Christians.

For 250 years the Roman Emperors tried to destroy Christianity through persecution. In the first 200 years of Christianity, every Pope but one was martyred—**the Romans certainly knew who the head of the Church was!**

A Roman Emperor's greatest fear was a rival to the throne. Nevertheless, the emperor Decius (249-251 A.D.), one of the harshest persecutors of the early Christian Church, made the following remark: "*I would far rather receive news of a rival to the throne than of another bishop of Rome.*"[22] Decius said this after he had executed Pope Fabian in 250 A.D.

REASON

Finally, appeal to reason. Ask Fundamentalists this question. Suppose that the owner of a company had called all the employees together and announced that he was going to be gone for a while. During his absence, he was going to give the keys of the company to John Doe and that whatever John Doe commanded would be backed by him. Would you have any doubt that John Doe was going to be in charge of the company while the boss was away? Of course not! Then why can't Fundamentalists accept that this is exactly what is described in **Mt 16:13-19**?

---

[20] St. Clement died about 80 A.D., some 20 years before the last Apostle, St. John, died. Although St. John was still alive in Ephesus, which was much closer to Corinth than was Rome, the Corinthians appealed to the Bishop of Rome because he had the "keys" of authority. Pope Clement wrote to the Church at Corinth: "*You, therefore, who laid the foundation of the rebellion, submit to the presbyters and be chastened to repentance, bending your knees in a spirit of humility.*" (*FIRST LETTER TO THE CORINTHIANS*, 57, 1; Jurgens, p. 12, #27.)
And again, "*If anyone disobey the things which have been said by Him through us, let them know that they will involve themselves in transgression and in no small danger.*" (*FIRST LETTER TO THE CORINTHIANS*, 59, 1; Jurgens, p. 12, #28a.)
[21] St. Irenaeus was bishop of Lyons from about 180-200 A.D. He is considered one of the greatest theologians of the immediate post-Apostolic period. In his work *AGAINST HERESIES*, St. Irenaeus makes the following statement about the Church of Rome and the successors of St. Peter: "*But since it would be too long to enumerate in such a small volume as this the successions of all the Churches, we shall confound all those who, in whatever manner, whether through self-satisfaction or vainglory, or through blindness and wicked opinion, assemble other than where it is proper, by pointing out here the successions of the bishops of the greatest and most ancient Church known to all, founded and organized at Rome by the two most glorious Apostles, Peter and Paul, that Church which has the tradition and the faith which comes down to us after having been announced to men by the Apostles. For with this Church, because of its superior origin, all the Churches must agree, that is, all the faithful in the whole*

---

world; and it is in her that the faithful everywhere have maintained the Apostolic tradition" (3, 3, 2; Jurgens, p. 90, #210). St. Irenaeus then goes on to name all the Popes succeeding Peter up to his time—twelve in all (3, 3, 3; Jurgens, p. 90, #211). The complete list of Popes from St. Peter to Pope John Paul II—264 in all—can be found in any public library.
[22] *CHRISTIAN HISTORY*, Issue 27 entitled "Persecution in the Early Church" (1990, Vol. IX, No. 3), p. 22.

MARIAN DOCTRINES

Fundamentalists think Catholics give too much honor to the Blessed Virgin Mary. They reject the four defined doctrines on Our Lady: (1) her **Divine Maternity** (that she is the Mother of God); (2) her **Perpetual Virginity** (that she remained a virgin throughout her entire life); (3) her **Bodily Assumption**; and (4) her **Immaculate Conception**.

Fundamentalists often want to discuss Marian beliefs immediately. Insist on starting with more **basic** differences: Apostolic authority, the Eucharist, or the "Bible alone" idea. However, you should be prepared to eventually discuss Marian doctrines.

Before beginning a discussion on the four major doctrines, ask Fundamentalists *why they think it is so wrong to honor the mother of our Savior*. Remind them that God honored her above all creatures by making her the mother of His Son. In honoring Mary, the Catholic Church is following the example of God Himself. Mary's special privileges were given to her by God, not men.

Read **Luke 1:26-56**. Note how the Archangel Gabriel shows Mary great honor in his greeting. See how Elizabeth, *"filled with the Holy Spirit,"* calls Mary blessed twice in just four short verses. Under the guidance of the Holy Spirit, Elizabeth gives Our Lady great honor with the words, *"And how does this happen to me, that the **mother of my Lord** should come to me?"*

In verse **48**, Our Lady prophesies that *all ages* will call her **blessed**. Ask Fundamentalists why they don't call her Blessed Virgin Mary as Catholics do. They call her Mary or perhaps Virgin Mary, but almost never *Blessed* Virgin Mary. Let them see that it is **Catholics** who are being biblical here and not Fundamentalists.

Once you have established the biblical basis for giving special honor to Our Lady, you can begin discussing the four major Marian doctrines. Don't try to deal with all four doctrines at once; this takes a lot of time and can involve many difficulties and side issues. For apologetic purposes **insist on focusing on Mary's title of Mother of God** for these reasons:

(1) This is her first and greatest privilege; the other privileges follow from this one. If they can understand and accept this doctrine, they will grasp the others more easily.

(2) It is the easiest to defend doctrinally, biblically, and historically.

(3) The three great pillars of the Reformation—Luther, Calvin, and Zwingli—all accepted this doctrine wholeheartedly.

Most Protestants are shocked to learn that although the founders of Protestantism rejected many Catholic doctrines, **they insisted on honoring Mary as Mother of God and Ever-Virgin** (see Appendix 2, page 20).

DOCTRINAL BASIS

All Christians believe that Jesus was born of the Blessed Virgin Mary. They also believe that although Jesus has two *natures* (one divine and one human), He is one Divine *Person*. Since this *one person* was born of Mary, she truly is the Mother of the **one Divine Person**: in short, the Mother of God.

If a person denies that Mary is the Mother of God, whether he realizes it or not, he is **denying the Incarnation**. He is saying either that Jesus is not God, or that Jesus is two persons—one human and one divine. Protestants ask: *How can Mary, a creature, be the mother of God the Creator?* We answer that when the eternal Son of God became man, He assumed a human nature, which made it possible for Him to be born of a woman just as we are.

BIBLICAL BASIS

(a) **Luke 1:43**: Elizabeth calls her *"mother of my Lord."* In the NT, "Lord" refers only to God.

(b) **Mt 1:23**: *"Behold the virgin shall be with child and bear a son, and they shall name Him Emmanuel,"* which means *"God is with us."*

(c) **Luke 1:35**: *"the child to be born will be called holy, the Son of God."*

(d) **Gal 4:4**: *"But when the fullness of time had come, God sent His Son, born of a woman."*

EARLY CHURCH FATHERS

*"For our **God, Jesus Christ, was conceived by Mary** in accord with God's plan...."*[23] (St. Ignatius, 110 A.D.)

*"The Virgin Mary, ... being obedient to His word, received from an angel the glad tidings that **she would bear God**."*[24] (St. Irenaeus, 180-199 A.D.)

Remind Protestants that if they look at Church history they will find that Mary's title of Mother of God was not rejected until 429 A.D. In that year a bishop named Nestorius promoted the heresy that Jesus was *two distinct persons*; and that Mary was only the mother of the human person. In 431 A.D., the Council of Ephesus condemned this heresy. It did not surface again in Christianity until after the Reformation. A correct belief about Mary leads to a correct belief about Jesus.

In regard to the other three Marian doctrines, biblical passages in support of them are not explicit and we have to rely on Apostolic Tradition and the teaching authority of the Church.

Assumption. The doctrine doesn't specify if Mary died; it merely states that after the completion of her life, she was taken body and soul into heaven. Note that Elijah and Enoch were assumed into heaven, just as the righteous will be at the end of time (see Gn 5:24; 2 Kg 2:11; 1 Thess 4:17; Heb 11:5). Why is it hard to believe that God gave His mother this privilege? No city ever claimed her body. There is no record of her relics or remains anywhere.

Immaculate Conception. The doctrine doesn't say that Mary didn't need a savior. Like all the OT saints, Mary was saved through the anticipated merits of Jesus. Mary's salvation was simply more perfect. By God's grace, she was *preserved* from sin at her conception. In contrast, we are *cleansed* from sin after our birth.

Perpetual Virginity. Mary's perpetual virginity was not challenged in the early Church until the time of St. Jerome (around 400 A.D.). This doctrine was *not rejected* by the founders of Protestantism. Note that "brothers" in the Bible can also mean "relatives." If Jesus had blood brothers, He

[23] *LETTER TO THE EPHESIANS*, 18, 2; Jurgens, p. 18, #42.
[24] *AGAINST HERESIES*, 5, 19, 1; Jurgens, p. 101, #256a.

would not have entrusted Mary to John, but to one of them. Two so-called "brothers" of Jesus (Mt 13:55)—James and Joseph—are identified as sons of another Mary, the wife of Clopas (compare Mt 27:56 and Jn 19:25).

APPENDIX 2: THE PROTESTANT REFORMERS' VIEW OF MARY

Luther, Calvin, and Zwingli, the three fathers of the Reformation, each affirmed the Catholic doctrines that Mary is the Mother of God and a Perpetual Virgin.

MARY AS MOTHER OF GOD

Martin Luther: "*In this work whereby she was made the **Mother of God**, so many and such good things were given her that no one can grasp them.... Not only was Mary the mother of Him who is born [in Bethlehem], but of Him who, before the world, was eternally born of the Father, from a Mother in time and at the same time man and God.*"[25]

John Calvin: "*It cannot be denied that God in choosing and destining Mary to be the Mother of His Son, granted her the highest honor.... Elizabeth calls Mary Mother of the Lord, because the unity of the person in the two natures of Christ was such that she could have said that **the mortal man engendered in the womb of Mary was at the same time the eternal God**.*"[26]

Ulrich Zwingli: "*It was given to her what belongs to no creature, that in the flesh **she should bring forth the Son of God**.*"[27] °

MARY AS PERPETUAL VIRGIN

Luther: "*It is an article of faith that Mary is Mother of the Lord and **still a virgin**.... Christ, we believe, came forth from a womb left perfectly intact.*"[28]

Calvin: "*There have been certain folk who have wished to suggest from this passage [Matt 1:25] that the Virgin Mary had other children than the Son of God, and that Joseph had then dwelt with her later; **but what folly this is**! For the gospel writer did not wish to record what happened afterwards; he simply wished to make clear Joseph's obedience and to show also that Joseph had been well and truly assured that it was God who had sent His angel to Mary. **He had therefore never dwelt with her nor had he shared her company**.... And besides this Our Lord Jesus Christ is called the first-born. This is not because there was a second or a third, but because the gospel writer is paying regard to the precedence. Scripture speaks thus of naming the first-born whether or no there was any question of the second.*"[29]

Zwingli: "*I firmly believe that Mary, according to the words of the gospel as a pure Virgin brought forth for us the Son of God and in childbirth and after childbirth **forever remained a pure, intact Virgin**.*"[30]

We should ask Fundamentalists to honor Mary as much as the founders of their own Protestant tradition did.

25 Weimer, The Works of Luther, English transl. by Pelikan, Concordia, St. Louis, v. 7, p. 572.
26 Calvini Opera, Corpus Reformatorum, Braunschweig-Berlin, 1863-1900, v. 45, p. 348, 35.

27 Zwingli Opera, Corpus Reformatorum, Berlin, 1905, in Evang. Luc., Op. comp., v. 6, I, p. 639.
28 Works of Luther, v. 11, pp. 319-320; v. 6, p. 510.
29 Sermon on Matthew 1:22-25, published 1562.
30 Zwingli Opera, v. 1, p. 424.

QUESTIONS ASKED ABOUT MARY

1. Why do Catholics adore Mary, who is just a human being?

Catholics do *not* adore Mary; we venerate and honor her. Why? The angel calls her "*full of grace*," and one who has "*found favor with God*" (Lk 1:28, 30 RSVCE); Elizabeth, filled with the Holy Spirit calls her "*blessed among women*" (v. 42); and Mary herself declares that "*all generations shall call me blessed*" (v. 48). Catholics, following Scripture, always call her blessed. Do you?

2. Why do Catholics call Mary the "Mother of God"? Wouldn't this mean Mary existed before God, or that she is older than God?

We call Mary Mother of God because she gave birth to Jesus, who is God. We follow the Spirit-filled Elizabeth who declared in Luke 1:43: "*how does this happen to me, that the **mother of my Lord** should come to me?*" Jesus is true God and true man: two *natures* in one undivided *Person*. By being the Mother of Jesus, Mary is also the Mother of God, the Second Person of the Holy Trinity. Mary did not give birth merely to a human nature, but to a person, the Son of God who took from her flesh a pure human nature. Lk 1:35: "***the child to be born** will be called holy, **the Son of God.**" Gal 4:4: "God sent His Son, **born of a woman.**" If Jesus is truly God-made-man, then Mary is truly the Mother of God. Obviously, Mary did not exist before God. Jesus is the Son of God from all *eternity*, who became also the Son of Mary in *time*.

3. Why do Catholics believe Mary was immaculately conceived? Romans 3:23 says that "ALL HAVE SINNED and are deprived of the glory of God."

Luke writes that Mary is full of grace, highly favored. Lk 1:37: "*For with God nothing shall be impossible.*" She is the "*woman*" of Gen 3:15 whose enmity with Satan and sin is absolute. She is the Ark of the Covenant (Ex 25:11-21) made to hold the *living* Word of God: a holy tabernacle made not of the purest gold, but of the purest flesh. St. Paul is emphasizing the universal aspect of sin extending to Jews and Gentiles alike. Babies have not sinned; Adam and Eve before the fall had not sinned; Jesus never sinned. These are some exceptions that fall outside St. Paul's condemnation. Mary is another.

4. If Mary never sinned, she doesn't need a Savior. So why does Mary say in Luke 1:47: "my spirit rejoices in God MY SAVIOR."

Mary was saved by the merits of Christ, just as we are. The difference between Mary and other Christians is that her salvation from sin was more perfect. While we are *freed* from original sin at our baptism, Mary was *preserved* from original sin at her conception. But Jesus is the Savior in both cases.

5. Why do Catholics believe that Mary was a Perpetual Virgin? Matt. 13:55-56 says that Jesus had brothers and sisters.

Catholics are not alone in this belief. Protestant Reformers Martin Luther, John Calvin, and Ulrich Zwingli also defended the perpetual virginity of Mary. The Hebrew and Aramaic languages spoken by Christ and His disciples do not have separate words for "brother," "cousin," or "near-relative." For example, in the original Hebrew, Lot is called Abraham's "brother" (Gen 14:14). Yet we know that Lot was Abraham's **nephew** (Gen 11:27). The Jews used the word "brother" for any near relative, without necessarily meaning "blood-brothers."

6. Why do Catholics believe that Mary was assumed body and soul into heaven?

Scripture does not record the Assumption of Mary, so we depend on Apostolic Tradition for our belief. However, the Assumption is not anti-scriptural. In fact, Scripture gives every indication that such a thing could occur. Consider the unusual ends of certain righteous people: Enoch, who was taken to heaven without dying (Heb 11:5); and Elijah, who was whisked into heaven by a fiery chariot (2 King 2:11). Matthew 27:52 suggests a bodily assumption before the Second Coming, and most Protestants believe in the "rapture" based on the events described in 1 Thess 4:17 and 1 Cor 15:52. Mary is simply the first to be "raptured."

7. Why did the Catholic Church invent the dogmas of the Immaculate Conception in 1854, and the Bodily Assumption in 1950?

The Catholic Church officially defined the doctrines in 1854 and 1950, respectively. She did not "invent" them at that time, any more than she "invented" the doctrine of the Trinity when she officially defined it in 325, or "invented" the New Testament when she officially determined the canon in 393 and 397. The Catholic Church was merely codifying a belief which always existed in the Church, and was expressed in the writings of the early Church Fathers.

8. Is a Catholic required to believe in the Immaculate Conception and Assumption of Mary?

Yes. All Catholics are required to believe *everything* that the Church teaches. Officially defined doctrines are called dogmas, which every Catholic must accept in order to be a faithful Catholic. When these two doctrines were infallibly defined, they became binding dogmas of faith.

9. Is a Catholic required to believe in the Church-approved apparitions of Mary, such as Fatima and Lourdes?

No. Catholics have the assurance of the Church that these revelations are orthodox and worthy of belief, but they are *not doctrine* or an addition to public revelation (which ended with the death of the last Apostle). Therefore a Catholic is free to accept or reject these officially approved apparitions.

10. Why do Catholics pray to Mary? 1 Tim 2:5 says "there is ONE mediator between God and man, the man Jesus Christ (RSVCE)."

Catholics ask for Mary's intercession for the same reason that we ask for a fellow Christian's intercession: "*the fervent prayer of a righteous person is very powerful*" (James 5:16). **Because** Jesus is the one mediator between earth and heaven, we intercede for one another as members of Christ's body. If fellow saints praying for us on earth do not destroy Christ's role as the one mediator, neither do glorified saints praying for us in heaven. Mary is the greatest saint. Why *wouldn't* you seek her powerful intercession?

11. Why do Catholics call Mary "Blessed" and honor her with prayers and devotions, like the Rosary?

Scripture calls her "blessed" and promises that all generations will invoke her by that title (see question 1). We honor Mary because of her great privileges: she was conceived without sin, became the mother of God while remaining a virgin, and was assumed bodily into heaven. There she reigns as queen of heaven and earth, mother of the Church, God's greatest creature, and mankind's greatest boast. We honor her because Jesus honored her (perfectly obeying the fourth commandment), and we are called to imitate Jesus.

12. Is the "Hail Mary" Scriptural?

Yes, the first part of the prayer is taken verbatim from Scripture. *"HAIL, FULL OF GRACE, THE LORD IS WITH YOU!"* (Luke 1:28). *"BLESSED ART THOU AMONG WOMEN, AND BLESSED IS THE FRUIT OF THY WOMB"* (v. 42)—JESUS. The second part is based on Scripture. HOLY MARY—*"you have found favor with God"* (v. 30)—MOTHER OF GOD—*"mother of my Lord"* (v. 43)—PRAY FOR US SINNERS—(as we pray for one another)—NOW AND AT THE HOUR OF OUR DEATH. AMEN.

13. Isn't the Rosary a kind of repetitious prayer condemned by Jesus in Mt 6:7?

In Mt 6:7, Jesus is not condemning all repeated prayers, only prayer repeated *"in the manner of the pagans."* Jesus is teaching Christians that they are not to pray with the pagan attitude that the more you repeat a prayer the more likely you are to be heard (see 1 Kings 18:25-29 for an example of this pagan mentality). A Christian who thinks he needs to repeat a prayer in order to be heard in heaven has a problem with faith. This is the error Jesus is correcting. Notice that Jesus repeats the same prayer three times in the Garden of Gethsemani (Mt 26:44). The publican who humbly repeated, *"O God, be merciful to me, a sinner"* (Lk 18:13) went home justified. The four living creatures in heaven repeat day and night, *"Holy, holy, holy is the Lord God Almighty, who was, and who is, and who is to come"* (Rev. 4:8). These verses show that prayer repeated with the proper attitude is very pleasing to God. The Rosary, recited devoutly, fulfills part of the biblical exhortation to *"pray without ceasing"* (1 Thess 5:17).

14. Aren't Catholics superstitious for believing that medals of Mary and relics of saints can perform miracles?

The Catholic Church teaches that only God can perform a true miracle. But we also know that God can act either directly or through secondary agents, like people. God sometimes even performs miracles through inanimate objects in order to show the intercessory power of a particular saint. A man came back to life when he contacted the bones of the holy prophet Elisha (2 Kings 13:20-21). God performed miraculous cures through Peter's shadow (Act 5:15-16) and through handkerchiefs that had touched St. Paul (Acts 19:11-12), showing the great intercessory power of St. Peter and St. Paul. Medals of Our Lady and relics of saints have no power to cause miracles in themselves. Rather, God performs miracles through these medals and relics to show the great intercessory power of Mary and the saints.

CONFESSION

Virtually all Protestants deny that Christ gave His disciples the power to forgive sins. To discuss the sacrament of confession well, you need to know **Jn 20:19-23**.

When Jesus bestowed on the disciples the power to forgive sins, He did it on Easter Sunday. This is significant because of the connection of the Resurrection with spiritual life. Notice that He conferred the power by *breathing* on the Apostles. The only other time that God breathed on anyone was when He breathed life into the first human being (Gn 2:7). Ask Fundamentalists to think about these powerful symbols and how they signify an awesome life-giving power given to the disciples. Note that Jesus gives the disciples the authority to forgive, **and not to forgive**. This means a priest has to *hear* the sins in order to know whether to forgive them or hold them bound.

Fundamentalists say they confess their sins to God while Catholics confess their sins only to priests. **Wrong.** Catholics always confess their sins to God. They do it *directly* as well as *through His ministers* because that is what God requires, as clearly taught in Scripture.

Know **2 Cor 5:17-20**. St. Paul explains how the Apostles are ambassadors of Christ's work of **reconciliation**. What does this mean but that they share in the ministry of Christ and forgive sins in His name? Also know **James 5:13-16**. James makes clear that the sins of the sick are forgiven in this sacrament of annointing. He specifies that the presbyters (priests) must be called. They obviously had a power the ordinary Christian did not: the power to forgive sins. Otherwise, why didn't James simply ask ordinary, fellow Christians to pray over the sick as is the case in numerous other passages?

Many Protestants believe that sins are wiped away in Baptism. This means they believe that their ministers are used by God as His *instruments in the forgiveness of sins* through a sacrament, Baptism, which they administer. Catholics believe that the priest is used by God as His instrument for the forgiveness of sins in three sacraments: Confession, Anointing, and Baptism. The disagreement here is not in principle. It is true that most Fundamentalists do not believe that sins are wiped away through Baptism. However, we can point out that they all believe that God can use *their* ministers as *instruments in His physical healing*. Why wouldn't God do the same with spiritual healing, which is more important?

Finally, return to **John 20:21**: "*As the Father has sent me, so I send you.*" The Apostles are to continue the mission of Christ. The essence of that mission is **THE FORGIVENESS OF SINS**. Jesus knows our human nature. He provided sacramental confession to give us several important gifts: humility, the certainty of forgiveness, spiritual direction, and help to overcome self-deception and rationalization in matters of sin.

Clearly, Christ gave His disciples the power to forgive sin. This power was intended to be passed on, since Christ knew people would sin until the end of time. Early Church history confirms that Christians believed this power *was* passed on to the Apostles' successors (see Jurgens: #493, #553, #602, #637, and #855a).

SCANDALS IN THE CHURCH

In the past several years, the Catholic Church in the United States has been hit with one scandal after another. Many of these crimes involve priests in acts of pedophilia. This is a hideous sin, and in priests it is truly an abomination. As a Catholic, you can be sure that you will be asked questions about this. How do you respond?

Acknowledge the situation honestly. Don't try to explain it away. Tell people that scandals have badly wounded the Church in this country. Also, admit that many mistakes have been made by our Church leaders in handling this issue. Now they are dealing with this problem in a forthright way. In some cases, the Vatican is directly intervening.

Many Fundamentalists will try to use these scandals to **attack celibacy**, and to **challenge the claim that the Catholic Church is the true Church**. You must be prepared to respond to both arguments.

CELIBACY

Celibacy has nothing to do with pedophilia or other sex scandals involving priests. *Most pedophiles are married men.* We are seeing pedophilia in major institutions everywhere, not just in the Catholic Church. Remind Fundamentalists that a few years ago we had one television evangelist after another involved in sex scandals, some involving perverted sex. All of these televangelists were *married*. **Nobody blamed these scandals on the institution of marriage!** Nobody demanded that Protestant ministers renounce marriage.

People do not get involved in sex scandals because they are married or celibate. They commit these sins because they fail God as individuals. You don't judge marriage by those who break their marriage vows. Neither should you judge celibacy by those who break their celibacy vows. *Marriage and celibacy should both be judged by those who are faithful to their vows.*

Remember, about one-half of all marriages break up. Does this mean that we should get rid of marriage? Of course not! It means we should work to strengthen married couples in their vocation. Similarly, the Church is not going to get rid of celibacy because a very few priests break their vows.

We know that marriage is a good thing because it was instituted by God, and made a sacrament by Christ. We know that celibacy is good because it was praised by Jesus (**Mt 19:10-12**), and strongly recommended by St. Paul for those who would devote themselves entirely to the ministry (**1 Cor 7:32-35**). We all know that millions of Christians have led saintly lives as both celibate and married people.

THE TRUE CHURCH

Scandals in the Church are *not* an argument against the Catholic claim to be the true Church. In the OT, we find baby sacrifice and temple prostitution involving leaders of the OT religion (Jer 32:32-35; 2 Kgs 23:7). Of the twelve Apostles, one betrayed Christ, one denied Him, one refused to believe in His Resurrection, and they all abandoned Him at the Garden of Gethsemani.

The Catholic Church is both human and divine. Because it is human, it will have scandals. Because it is divine, it will last forever. Scandals are found in all denominations; they have nothing to do with the Catholic Church being the true Church.

What St. Paul wrote concerning the Jews applies also to Christians: *"What if some were unfaithful? Will their infidelity nullify the fidelity of God? Of course not!"* (Rom 3:3-4). Christ's faithfulness to His Church remains even when some of its members are unfaithful (see 2 Tim 2:13).

Scandals do not prove that the Catholic Church is false. They only prove what is obvious: that the Church contains **sinners as well as saints**, tares along with the wheat. In the parable of the wheat and the weeds (Mt 13:24-30), Our Lord makes clear that good and evil will exist side by side until the end of time. Mt 13:47-48 also confirms that the Church contains good and bad members alike.

PRAYER TO THE SAINTS

Is it biblical to ask the saints in heaven to pray for us? Catholics say yes, since we are all part of the *communion of saints*. Most Protestants say no, even though many of them recite the Apostles' Creed. Thus, they profess to believe in the "communion of saints," but usually they cannot explain what this means. What *does* it mean to believe in the **communion of saints**? Does this belief give us the biblical foundations for the doctrine of **intercessory prayer**?

COMMUNION OF SAINTS

As the word suggests, the *communion* of saints refers to the bond of unity among all believers, both living and dead, who are committed followers of Christ. In Christ, we are made part of God's family (1 Tim 3:15), children of God (1 John 3:1), joint heirs with Christ (Rom 8:17), and partakers of the divine nature (2 Pet 1:4). This family communion of saints is known to Catholics as the **Mystical Body of Christ**.[31] We are joined in a supernatural union as members of Christ's own body, and thus as members of one another. Each of us participates in the divine life of Christ Himself.

Know the image of **the Vine and the Branches** (John 15:1-5). Remind non-Catholics that because we as branches are connected to Christ the vine, *we are also connected to each other*. It is the life and grace of Jesus that gives us life and unites us in our common pilgrimage to heaven.

St. Paul emphasizes this unity in Christ's body in **1 Cor 12:12-27** (especially v. **25-27**) and in **Rom 12:4-16.** Know these passages.

INTERCESSORY PRAYER

What we have said about the communion of saints gives us the biblical reasons why Catholics ask the saints to intercede for them:

(1) **All Christians are members of Christ's body and one another** (Rom 12:5 and many others).

(2) **Jesus has only one body** (Eph 4:4; Col 3:15).

(3) **Death cannot separate Christians from Christ or from one another** (Rom 8:35-39).

(4) **Christians are bound in mutual love** (Rom 12:10; 1 Thess 5:11; Gal 6:2).

We are members of Christ's one body, united in His divine life even beyond the grave, and concerned with each other's salvation and growth in God's family. In that union, we call for help and support from our older brothers and sisters who have already won their crown of glory.

Just as in our human families we naturally turn to our siblings for aid and example, how much more should we turn to our supernatural family for help and inspiration.

Several objections are directed against the Catholic position on intercessory prayer.

OBJECTION 1: *The saints are dead. Catholics practice necromancy, communication with the dead, which is condemned (Dt 18:10-11).*

[31] The teaching that the Church is the Body of Christ is found throughout the NT: 1 Cor 10:16; Gal 3:28; Eph 1:22-23, 4:4, 4:15-16, 5:21-32; Col 1:18, 3:15.

Answer: Necromancy means summoning forth spirits from the shadowy underworld (OT "Sheol"), in order to converse with them. By asking the saints in heaven to intercede for us, Catholics are not conjuring roaming spirits or communicating in any "spiritualistic" way. So prayer to the saints has nothing to do with necromancy.

Nor are the saints dead. The saints in heaven are **alive** and **with God**: "*He is not God of the dead, but of the living*" (Mk 12:26-27). In Mark 9:4, Jesus is seen conversing with Elijah and Moses. Jesus tells the Good Thief: "*Amen, I say to you, **today** you will be with me in Paradise*" (Lk 23:43). In fact, **the saints in heaven are more alive than we are.** They are free from all sin. They enjoy the fullness of God's life-giving presence. Flooded with God's love, they care more about us now than they did on earth.

Just as Paul asked fellow believers (saints) to pray for him (Rom 15:30; Col 4:3; 1 Thess 5:25; Eph 6:18-19; 2 Thess 3:1), now we can ask Paul and the other saints in heaven to pray for us. We are not cut off from each other at death, rather we are brought closer through the communion we share in Christ.

We know that angels and saints place the prayers of the holy ones at God's feet (Tob 12:12; Rev 5:8; Rev 8:3-4), supporting those prayers with their intercessions. The martyrs underneath the heavenly altar cry out for earthly vindication (Rev 6:9-11), showing they are aware of, and concerned with, earthly affairs. The angels and saints in heaven will intercede for us before the throne of God if they are petitioned in prayer.

OBJECTION 2: *1 Tim 2:5 says there is one mediator between God and man. Isn't prayer to the saints in violation of 1 Tim 2:5?*

Answer: 1 Tim 2:5 must be understood in the light of 1 Peter 2:5: "*let yourselves be built into a spiritual house, to be a **holy priesthood, to offer spiritual sacrifices** acceptable to God **through Jesus Christ**.*" St. Peter says that Christians share in the one, eternal priesthood of Jesus Christ. Jesus is mediator between God and man **because** of His priesthood. Therefore, *to share in Christ's priesthood means to share in His mediatorship*, both in heaven and on earth.

1 Tim 2:5 confirms that we share in Christ's mediation, when we read it *in context*. In verses 1-7, St. Paul asks Christians to participate in Christ's unique mediation by offering prayers and intercessions for all men: "*this is good and pleasing to God.*" We are called to unite ourselves to the one mediator Christ, "*who gave himself as a ransom for all,*" by praying *for* all men, *through* Christ.

Because Christians share in the priesthood of Christ, **we share in a lesser and dependent way in His unique mediation**, interceding for all men.

Fellow Christians on earth intercede for each other in prayer *without contradicting the unique mediation of Jesus Christ*. Likewise, there is no contradiction of 1 Tim 2:5 if the saints in heaven intercede for us with their prayers. All prayer, whether in heaven or on earth, is *in* Christ and *through* Christ, our one mediator and high priest.

The principle is this: although God alone possesses all perfections, **we can participate in God's perfections by sharing in His divine life.** For example, the Bible says *only* God is good (Mk 10:18). Yet we can share in that absolute Goodness: "*Well done, my **good** and faithful servant*" (Mt 25:23).

Jesus shares many of His unique roles with Christians in lesser ways. Jesus is the **Creator** of all things (Jn 1:3; Col 1:16-17), and yet He shares this role with men and women in procreation. Jesus is the only **Shepherd** (Jn 10:11-16), yet He delegates this role to St. Peter (Jn 21:15-16) and later to others (Eph 4:11). Jesus is the eternal **High Priest**, mediating His once-for-all sacrifice for our redemption (Heb 3:1, 7:24, 9:12, 10:12), and yet Christians are also called to join in Christ's priesthood, as we have seen (1 Pet 2:5; Rev 1:6, 5:10).

Obviously, Christ is the unique and primary Creator, Shepherd, and Priest, but **each Christian participates in these roles in subordinate ways**. By sharing Christ's divine life, Christians also share in Christ's role as the only mediator.

OBJECTION 3: *The saints in heaven can't hear us.*

Answer: Why not? Aren't they more alive now than when they were with us? The medium of communication is Christ himself—the vine between the branches. We and the saints form one communion, one body of Christ, being members of Him and members of one another. Heb 12:1 tells us that we are surrounded by *"a cloud of witnesses."* How could those watching be unconcerned about our welfare? Look at Rev 5:8 and Rev 8:3. The petitions offered as incense to God must be for those who still need help, the holy ones on earth. They are offered by those who can help the most, the holy ones in heaven.

In the parable of Lazarus and the rich man (Lk 16:19-30), the departed rich man is able to pray to Abraham and intercede for his brothers. This implies that there can be communication across the abyss, and that fraternal charity extends beyond the grave.

We are certain that the saints in heaven enjoy the face to face vision of God (1 Cor. 13:12; 1 Jn 3:2). It is in this vision that they are aware of our prayers to them.

OBJECTION 4: *How can saints hear all these prayers, from all different people, all the time? It must sound like a deafening babble.*

Answer: Heaven has no space or time. Everything appears to God as *one eternal present*. Like God, the saints are outside of the limitations of space and time. Our earthly way of knowing is limited and incomplete. *"At present, we see indistinctly, as in a mirror, but then face to face. At present I know partially; **then I shall know fully, as I am fully known**"* (1 Cor 13:12). Our heavenly way of knowing is full and perfect.

PURGATORY

In order to defend the doctrine of Purgatory, you must explain two preliminary distinctions: (1) between **guilt** and **punishment**; and (2) between **mortal** and **venial** sin.

Does God forgive the GUILT of sin and still require PUNISHMENT (reparation, atonement, expiation)?

Ask King David. In 2 Sam 12:13-14 we read: *"David said to Nathan, 'I have sinned against the Lord.' Nathan answered David, 'The Lord on His part has **forgiven your sin**: you shall not die. **But** since you have utterly spurned the Lord by this deed, **the child born to you must surely die.'"** God forgave the guilt of David's sin, but He still required reparation in the form of suffering. A man might forgive a teenager for breaking his window, but still insist that he repair the damages.

Where does Scripture distinguish between MORTAL and VENIAL sin?

1 Jn 5:16-17 proves degrees of sin, distinguishing between *deadly sin* and sin that is *not deadly*. James 1:14-15 reads: *"each person is tempted when he is lured and enticed by his own desire. Then **desire conceives and brings forth sin, and when sin reaches maturity it gives birth to death**."* St. James distinguishes desire from sin, and *beginning sin* from *mature sin* which brings death. Sin which brings death to the soul is **mortal.** Sin which only wounds and disfigures the soul is **venial.**

What if you die with only venial sins?

The souls of those who die in the perfect state of grace, without the least sin or reparation due to sin, go directly to heaven. The souls of those who die in the state of unrepented mortal (deadly) sin go directly to hell. What about the middle sort of people: **those who die in the state of grace, but with venial sin or with unpaid reparation due to forgiven sin**? They do not merit hell: they are still in the state of grace; yet they are not pure enough for heaven, where *"nothing unclean will enter"* (Rev. 21:27).

What does the Bible say about this?

God is perfect holiness.

Is 6:3: *"'Holy, holy, holy is the Lord of hosts!' they [the Seraphim] cried one to the other."*

We are called to that same holiness.

Mt 5:48: *"So be perfect, just as your heavenly Father is perfect."*

1 Pet 1:15-16: *"...as he who called you is holy, be holy yourselves in every aspect of your conduct, for it is written, 'Be holy because I am holy.'"*

Without perfect holiness, we cannot see God in heaven.

Heb 12:14: *"Strive for peace with everyone, and for that holiness without which no one will see the Lord."*

Rev 21:27: *"...nothing unclean will enter it [heaven]."*

What happens to the faithful who die without perfect holiness or with sin that is not deadly? The biblical, logical, and historical answer is **Purgatory.**

Purgatory comes from the verb "purge" meaning "to purify or cleanse." We should keep this notion of **purification** in mind when explaining this doctrine.

What is the Catholic belief about Purgatory?

Purgatory is a temporary state of purification for the imperfect saints. The souls of the just who have died in the state of grace but with venial sins or with reparation due for forgiven mortal and venial sins are fully cleansed in Purgatory so that they may enter heaven. In Purgatory all remaining reparation for sin is made; all remaining self-love is purged and purified until only love of God remains.

Remember these three points:

(1) Only **imperfect saints in the state of grace** enter Purgatory. It is not a "second chance" for those who die in unrepented mortal sin.

(2) Purgatory exists for **purification** and **reparation**. The effects of sin are purged. The punishments due to sin are paid.

(3) Purgatory is only **temporary**. Once the imperfect saints are purified they enter heaven. Everyone in Purgatory will go to heaven. Purgatory will then cease to exist. Only heaven and hell will remain eternally.

Is Purgatory Scriptural?

First, we should note that the word "purgatory" is not found in Sacred Scripture. This is not the point. The words "Trinity" and "Incarnation" are not found in Scripture, yet these doctrines are clearly taught there. Likewise, **the Bible teaches that an intermediate state of purification exists**. We call it Purgatory. What is

important is the doctrine, not the name.

Where is the doctrine of Purgatory referred to in the Bible?

Mt 12:32: "*And whoever speaks a word against the Son of Man will be forgiven; but whoever speaks against the Holy Spirit will not be forgiven, either in this age or in the age to come.*" Jesus implies that **some sins can be forgiven in the next world**. Sin cannot be forgiven in Hell. There is no sin to be forgiven in heaven. Any remission of sin in the next world can only occur in Purgatory.

1 Cor 3:15: "*But if someone's work is burned up, that one will suffer loss; the person will be saved, but only as through fire.*" This cannot refer to eternal loss in hell, for there no one is saved. Nor can it refer to heaven, for there no one suffers. It refers, then, to a middle state where the soul temporarily suffers loss so that it may gain heaven. This is essentially the definition of Purgatory.

1 Pet 3:18-20: "*For Christ also suffered for sins once, the righteous for the sake of the unrighteous, that he might lead you to God. Put to death in the flesh, he was brought to life in the spirit. In it he also went to preach to the spirits in prison, who had once been disobedient while God patiently waited in the days of Noah during the building of the ark, in which a few persons, eight in all, were saved through water.*"

1 Peter 4:6: "*For this is why the gospel was preached even to the dead that, though condemned in the flesh in human estimation, they might live in the spirit in the estimation of God.*" Note that it is a **prison for disobedient spirits**, and yet they were **saved** when Jesus preached to them. This is not hell, because no one is saved from hell. This is probably not the "limbo of the fathers," (often called "Abraham's bosom," where the righteous souls of the OT waited until Christ opened the gates of heaven), because this is a place for **disobedient** spirits. One cannot imagine that St. Peter is describing the waiting place of such righteous OT saints as David and John the Baptist when he mentions disobedient spirits.

St. Peter is describing a temporary state for disobedient souls who were eventually saved. *At the very least, it proves that a third place can exist between heaven and hell.* At the very most, it proves the Catholic doctrine of Purgatory.

The clearest affirmation of the existence of Purgatory comes from the Greek Septuagint: the Old Testament Scriptures used by Christ, all the NT writers, and the councils of Hippo and Carthage (which authoritatively determined the "canon" of inspired books of the Bible).

2 Maccabees 12:44-46: "*...for if he were not expecting the fallen to rise again, it would have been useless and foolish to pray for them in death. But if he did this with a view to the splendid reward that awaits those who had gone to rest in godliness, it was a holy and pious thought. Thus* **he made atonement for the dead that they might be freed from this sin**.*"* It is impossible to aid souls in heaven (they have no need), and equally impossible to aid souls in hell (they have no hope). Praying for the dead presumes souls in a middle state where atonement for sin can be made.

This passage from Maccabees is a PROOF text. *It explicitly affirms an intermediate state where the faithful departed make atonement for their sins.* 2 Maccabees was so contrary to the "justification by faith alone" theology of the Reformers that Martin Luther chose to remove it (along with six other books) from the Old Testament.

This takes us back to the question of the canon of the Bible: *How do you know which books* **really** *constitute the Bible?* **By whose authority** do you trust that the books upon which you stake your eternal salvation *really are inspired*?

Do you rely on the private judgment of a renegade priest, Luther, who also wanted to throw out Esther, James and Revelation, and thought nothing of adding a word to his translation of Romans?

OR, do you accept the divinely-protected judgment of the Catholic Church who used her authority around the year 400 A.D. to determine the official canon of the Bible. This is the same Bible (less seven books) used by the Protestants to attack the very authority of the Church who gave it to them.

Even if 2 Maccabees is rejected as Scripture, there can be no doubt that, *as history*, **the book accurately reflects the religious character of the Jews of the second century BC**. A little more than one hundred years before Christ, *Jews prayed for their dead* (and still do today).

In fact, some of the earliest Christian liturgies (worship services) include prayers for the dead. Ancient Christian tomb inscriptions from the second and third centuries frequently contain an appeal for prayers for the dead.[32] This practice makes sense *only if early Christians believed in Purgatory* even if they did not use that name for it.

Tertullian, writing in the year 211 A.D., presents the practice of praying and sacrificing for the dead as an established custom: "*We offer sacrifices for the dead on their birthday anniversaries.*"[33] The practice of praying for the dead was universal among Christians for fifteen centuries before the Reformation.

Are there any New Testament passages that refer to prayers and practices performed for the benefit of the deceased?

2 Tim 1:16-18: "*May the Lord grant mercy to the family of Onesiphorus because he often gave me new heart and was not ashamed of my chains.... May the Lord grant him to find mercy from the Lord on that day.*" St. Paul prays for his departed friend Onesiphorus, which makes sense only if he can be helped by prayer.

I Cor 15: 29-30: "*Otherwise, what will people accomplish by having themselves baptized for the dead? If the dead are not raised at all, then why are they having themselves baptized for them?*" In his argument for the resurrection of the body, St. Paul mentions (without condemning or approving) the practice of people having themselves baptized for the benefit of the dead, who cannot be helped if there is no intermediate state of purification.[34]

In short, if the Jews, St. Paul, and the early Christians prayed for the dead, we should have no fear of praying for them as well. Praying for the dead *presumes an intermediate state of purification*, whatever you may call it. Catholics call it Purgatory.

---

[32] The epitaph of Abercius [180 AD] reads: "*The citizen of a prominent city, I erected this while I lived, that I might have a resting place for my body. Abercius is my name, a disciple of the chaste shepherd who feeds his sheep on the mountains and in the fields, who has great eyes surveying everywhere, who taught me the faithful writings of life. Standing by, I, Abercius ordered this to be inscribed; truly I was in my seventy second year. May everyone who is in accord with this and who understands it pray for Abercius*" (Jurgens, p. 78, #187).

---

[33] *THE CROWN,* 3, 3; Jurgens, p. 151, #367.

[34] On the grounds of sola scriptura, Protestants have no way to refute the Mormon practice of baptism for the dead. They must have recourse to the Fathers and Church Tradition to prove that Christianity never endorsed this practice.

MISCELLANEOUS QUESTIONS

1. Why do Catholics call their priests "father," when Jesus commands us in Matthew 23:9 to "call no man father?"

In Matthew 23:1-12, when Jesus tells us to call no man "father" or "teacher," He is using figurative language to emphasize that all legitimate authority and truth ultimately come from God. We are not to take these passages literally.

Throughout the Bible men are called fathers and teachers. Both Catholics and Protestants call earthly men fathers and teachers. St. Stephen and St. Paul call the Jewish religious leaders "fathers" (Acts 7:2 and 22:1). St. Paul calls the Corinthians "*my beloved children.... for I became your father in Christ Jesus through the Gospel*" (1 Cor 4:14-15; also see 1 Thess 2:11, 1 Tim 1:2, and Tit 1:4). St. Paul became their spiritual father because he cooperated with God in giving them spiritual life, just as biological fathers cooperate with God in giving physical life. Catholics call their priests "father" because, like St. Paul, priests cooperate with God in giving spiritual life to their flock by preaching the Gospel and administering the sacraments.

2. Why do Catholics worship statues in violation of Exodus 20:4-5?

Catholics certainly don't worship statues, or anything created. The Catholic Church teaches that **only** God is to be worshipped: to worship anything created is to commit the serious sin of idolatry. In Ex 20:4-5, God prohibits the making of images *for the purpose of worshipping them*. **But God does not prohibit image-making altogether**. In Ex 25:18-19, God commands Moses to make statues of angels (cherubim). In Num

21:8, God tells Moses to make a bronze serpent (seraph), which the Israelites had to look upon in order to be healed. The Jews also used many carved images in the Temple, including cherubim, oxen, lions, palm trees, and flowers (1 Kings 6 and 7).

Catholics use statues and other images to call to mind the holy people they represent: Jesus, the angels, and the saints. For the same reason, Protestants use Christmas nativity scenes to depict the same holy people: Jesus, the angels, and the saints. Catholics simply use statues and images in devotions all year around.

The rejection of statues and other images in Church devotional life is a heresy known as "iconoclasm." It was first seen in Christianity in the eighth century when the wicked Emperor Leo the Isaurian, influenced by the new religion of Islam (founded in 622 A.D.), began attacking the use of statues and icons in the Church. In the Second Council of Nicea in 787 A.D., the Church condemned this heresy. It did not resurface in Christianity until the Reformation.

3. Didn't the Catholic Church become pagan after Constantine became emperor?

Constantine's Christian mother, St. Helena, raised him with Christian beliefs (although he delayed baptism until his deathbed). He defeated the pagan general Maxentius under the standard of the Christian cross in 312 A.D. The next year Constantine signed the Edict of Milan which officially ended the Roman persecution of the Church. It is absurd to think he attempted to paganize the Church. In 361 A.D., the emperor Julian the Apostate launched a persecution of the Church in an attempt to bring back paganism. This would not have been necessary if the Church had become pagan at the time of Constantine (312-337 A.D.). A careful study of the first 300 years of Christianity reveals that Catholic doctrines such as the Eucharist, Apostolic authority, and the Pope as the successor of St. Peter, were believed by Christians from the very beginning. They certainly did not arise after Constantine.

4. Is the Mass really a sacrifice?

Fundamentalists reject the Catholic teaching on the Holy Sacrifice of the Mass for two reasons. They claim the Mass violates many passages in Hebrews which tell us Jesus was only *sacrificed once*, and that, *without the shedding of blood*, there is no forgiveness of sins (Heb 9:22, 25, 28, 10:11-12). They think Catholics teach Jesus is sacrificed *again* at every Mass. They cite Catholic catechisms which teach that in the Mass Jesus is offered in an *unbloody manner.*

The Catholic Church teaches that the **one, all-sufficient, bloody sacrifice** of Jesus at Calvary is **made present** at each Mass in an unbloody manner. Christ is not re-sacrificed at each Mass; rather the Mass re-presents the one sacrifice of Calvary. Thus, the efficacy (effectiveness) of the Mass comes entirely from the one, bloody sacrifice of Calvary.

The passages referred to in Hebrews compare the many sacrifices of the OT religion, which could not atone for sin nor reconcile mankind to God, with the one sacrifice of Christ which did atone for all sins and reconcile mankind to God. Hebrews also stresses that the bloody sacrifices of animals in the OT prefigured the bloody sacrifice of Christ for the remission of sin.

The Mass, also known as the Lord's Supper or the Eucharist, repeats what happened at the Last Supper. At the Last Supper Our Lord turned bread into His body, and said that this body would be offered up (sacrificed) for us. He turned wine into His blood, and said that this blood would be shed (sacrificed) for us. Clearly, at the Last Supper, Jesus made His future sacrifice at Calvary present. He then commanded His disciples to repeat this mystery. In 1 Cor 11:26, St. Paul tells us that in the celebration of the Eucharist we *"proclaim the death of the Lord until He comes."* Thus, the Last Supper, which made the sacrifice of Calvary present, will continue to be repeated in the Mass until the end of time. In this way, Christ's once-for-all sacrifice will be made present to the faithful until the end of time.

5. Does baptism regenerate, or is it only a symbolic washing?

Most Fundamentalists believe that baptism is only a symbolic washing—an ordinance, not a sacrament. Catholics believe that baptism is a sacrament of the NT instituted by Christ. Catholics believe that through baptism all sin, original and actual, is wiped away. The life of God, called sanctifying grace, is infused into the soul, and a person is born again of *water* and the Holy Spirit (Jn 3:5). Jesus made baptism a condition for entering heaven (Jn 3:5; Mk 16:16). In Acts 2:38, St. Peter says that through baptism our sins are forgiven and we receive the Holy Spirit. St. Paul says that we are given new life (regeneration) through baptism (Rom 6:4). Titus 3:5 tells us that we are saved *"by the **washing of regeneration** and renewal in the Holy Spirit* (RSVCE)," which refers to baptism. 1 Peter 3:20-21 says that *"baptism ... **saves you now**."*

In essence, Fundamentalists confuse the baptism of Jesus with the baptism of John the Baptist. John's baptism was only a symbolic washing. However, John says that Jesus' baptism would give the Holy Spirit, whereas his own did not (Mt 3:11). At the time of the Reformation, many Protestants rejected baptism as a sacrament of regeneration because it did not fit with their new and unorthodox notion of justification by faith alone.

Jesus would not have made baptism a condition for entering heaven if it were only symbolic. The writings of the early Church Fathers show that they all taught that water baptism regenerates. The idea that baptism is only a symbolic washing arose centuries later with the Reformation.

6. Why do Catholics baptize infants?

Fundamentalists believe that baptism is only a symbolic washing signifying that a person has accepted Jesus as his Lord and Savior. According to them, since an infant cannot accept Jesus as Lord and Savior (because he does not have the use of reason), baptism is meaningless for him.

However, Jesus requires baptism for entering heaven (Jn 3:5; Mk 16:16). St. Paul tells us that all are born with Adam's sin and thus need baptism (Rom 5:18-19). Jesus makes clear that children are not to be kept away from Him (Mk 10:14). The Apostles baptized entire households (Acts 16:15, 33; 1 Cor 1:16). This would include infants. No Bible passage prohibits infant baptism.

The early Church Fathers were clear that the baptizing of infants was a practice that came from the Apostles themselves. That infants lack the use of reason does not prevent them from becoming part of the New Covenant through baptism. In the OT, a child became part of the Old Covenant through circumcision. This was done eight days after birth, long before the child could choose for himself whether or not to be part of the Chosen People. Just as parents in the OT supplied the decision for the child's circumcision until he could confirm this decision at the age of reason, so in the NT parents stand in for the child at his baptism until he can confirm this decision at the age of reason.

7. Aren't we saved by faith alone as St. Paul says in Romans 3:28?

When St. Paul says, "*For we consider that a person is justified by faith **apart from works of the law**,*" he is teaching that the works of the OT Mosaic law, such as circumcision, could not bring salvation. In the NT, faith does bring salvation, provided it is made alive by charity. Saving faith is **active**: it is "*faith **working** through love*" (Gal 5:6).

In 1 Cor 13:2, St. Paul tells us that faith without love (charity) is nothing (it cannot save). Charity means love of God, and Jesus says that if we love Him, we will keep His commandments (Jn 14:21). When the rich man asks Jesus what he must do to be saved, Jesus answers: "*keep the commandments*" (Mt. 19:16-17). Thus it is clear from Scripture that faith alone is not enough for salvation. We must also have charity and keep God's commandments.

St. James condemns the idea that we are saved by faith *apart* from good works: "*See how a person is justified by works and **not by faith alone.**[35] ... For just as a body without a spirit is dead, so also **faith without works is dead**"* (Jam 2:24, 26).

The Catholic Church teaches that we are saved by God's grace alone. Grace enables us to have the saving faith that works in love (Eph 2:8-10). All good works must be done in the grace of God to have any supernatural value.

8. If the redemptive work of Christ is all-sufficient, why do Catholics insist on various good works and penances?

Fundamentalists think that because Catholics teach salvation depends on faith *and* good works, Catholics must not believe the redemptive work of Christ is sufficient. They see good works, penances, Purgatory, prayer to the saints, and the sacraments, as unnecessary additions to the **completed** work of Christ. Fundamentalists have this notion because they confuse salvation with redemption.

Catholics firmly agree with Protestants that the redemptive work of Christ is complete and all-sufficient. Through His suffering, death, and resurrection, Jesus **redeemed everyone**: He paid for all sins and made it *possible* for anyone to be saved. However, we know that not everyone is *automatically* saved.

All Christians admit that people can fail to be saved by refusing to repent, or by refusing to cooperate with God's grace in others areas. Although the redemptive work of Christ is complete, *the merits of His redemption must still be **applied** to each*

person in order for him to be saved. Thus, a person must repent (Mt 4:17), believe in Jesus (Acts 16:31), keep the commandments (Mt 19:16-17), and live a life of charity (1 Cor 13:1-3), as Scripture plainly teaches. A Catholic who performs good works in Christ isn't denying the completed work of Christ's redemption; he is depending on it.

9. Can you lose your salvation once you accept Jesus as Lord and Savior?

Most, though not all, Fundamentalists believe that once you accept Jesus as your Lord and Savior, it is impossible to lose your salvation. This doctrine is known as "once saved, always saved." Like many other Protestant doctrines, this teaching was unheard of before the Reformation.

Mt 24:13 tells us that we must *"persevere to the end"* in order to be saved. St. Paul says the same thing in 2 Tim 2:12: that we must hold out to the end if we want to reign with Christ. In Rom 11:22, Christians are warned that they will be cut off if they don't persevere in the kindness of God. Hebrews 6:4-6 describes people who are sharers in the Holy Spirit (born-again Christians) but then fall away from God.

Remember St. Paul's advice: *"work out your salvation with fear and trembling"* (Phil 2:12). Who should have more assurance of salvation than St. Paul? Yet he says: *"I drive my body and train it, for fear that, after having preached to others, I myself should be disqualified"* (1 Cor 9:27). Scripture is very clear: Christians **can** lose their salvation.

The Catholic Church teaches we must die in sanctifying grace in order to be saved. Any mortal sin leads to a loss of sanctifying

---

[35]Luther's battle cry, "justification by faith alone," is expressly contradicted by Scripture, which explains why he called the book of James (a part of God's infallible Word) "an epistle of straw."

grace and the risk of eternal damnation if we should die in this state.

10. Why does the Catholic Church base some of its doctrines on tradition instead of basing them all on the Bible? Isn't tradition condemned in the Bible (Mt 15:3; Mk 7:9; Col 2:8)?

Fundamentalists think **all** tradition is condemned in Scripture. But the Bible speaks of two kinds of tradition: human and apostolic. Bad human tradition *is* condemned. In Mt 15:3 and Mk 7:9, Jesus clearly condemns human tradition that sets aside the commandments of God. In Col 2:8, St. Paul tells us to beware of false reasoning "*according to* **human tradition**." But in condemning erroneous human traditions (small "t"), neither Jesus nor St. Paul is condemning Apostolic Traditions (capital "T"), the deposit of divine truths that Jesus orally entrusted to the Apostles.

The Bible actually commands following Apostolic Traditions. St. Paul *commends* the Corinthians for following apostolic traditions (1 Cor 11:2). St. Paul *commands* the Thessalonians to keep them: "*Therefore, brothers, stand firm and hold fast to the* **traditions** *that you were taught, either by an* **oral statement** *or by a* **letter** *of ours*" (2 Thess 2:15; see also 2 Thess 3:6). Obeying St. Paul, the Church bases its doctrines on Sacred Scripture *and* Apostolic Tradition.

11. Hasn't the Catholic Church changed its doctrines through the years?

Fundamentalists often accuse the Catholic Church of changing its doctrines, or inventing new ones. Usually they are confusing Church **doctrines** with Church **disciplines**. A doctrine is an unchangeable truth revealed by God—such as the Virgin Birth, while a discipline is a changeable regulation—like the priest facing the people instead of the altar during the Mass.

The Catholic Church teaches there can be *no new doctrines* since the death of the last apostle. The Apostolic deposit of faith was delivered once and for all (Jude 3). The eternal truths of God must be lived out in different times, cultures, and places. Church disciplines which help us live out these truths are therefore adapted as conditions in the Church change.

We must also remember that doctrines can *develop*, in the sense of being understood more fully and made more explicit. These fuller insights are passed on by the Church through its teaching office (Magisterium). This is not invention, but proper growth. Whenever a Fundamentalist insists that the Catholic Church has changed its doctrines, you can be sure that he has either confused a discipline with a doctrine, or else mistaken true doctrinal development for a new invention.

12. Why does the Catholic Church forbid its priests to marry? Doesn't St. Paul call forbidding marriage a "doctrine of devils" (1 Tim 4:1-3)?

The Catholic Church does not forbid marriage; the Church upholds the great dignity of marriage. Marriage is considered a holy sacrament that symbolizes the union of Christ with His Church (Eph 5:21-33). The Church only forbids marriage, as a matter of discipline, to those men who choose to become priests. No one is forced into the priesthood. Those who wish to become priests are asked to renounce sex for the sake of the kingdom of God.

Remember, Jesus praises those who would freely renounce sex for the kingdom of God (Mt 19:12).

St. Paul's denunciation of those who forbid marriage applies to those who reject marriage **entirely**, as though it were an evil in itself. St. Paul is warning against a false spirituality which holds that any part of God's good creation (including marriage) is evil (1 Tim 4:3-4).

St. Paul obviously is not condemning celibacy. St. Paul was himself single (1 Cor 7:8), just as Jesus was. St. Paul strongly *recommends* celibacy for those who would devote themselves entirely to the ministry (1 Cor 7:32-35). Since St. Paul does not absolutely *command* celibacy for all full-time ministers, the Catholic Church teaches the requirement of celibacy is a **discipline**, not a **doctrine**. Thus, the Church allows certain exceptions to this requirement: for example, married Anglican priests who become Catholic can continue to be married even if they become Catholic priests.

Ask Fundamentalists why *they* have so *few*, if any, celibate ministers, especially since St. Paul encourages it so strongly for full-time ministers of Christ.

13. Does it make any difference which Christian denomination I join?

Although it is very clear in Scripture and early Church history that Christ left only *one* Church, today we have over 25,000 Christian denominations. Does it matter which of these you join? It most certainly does! If Christ founded only one Church, then all the other Christian churches were founded *by men*. Although they believe much that is true, and have many members who are sincere Christians, we simply cannot

choose any of them over the Church founded by Christ.

14. How do we determine which is the Church founded by Christ?

The Church founded by Christ must go back in **history** to the time of Christ; its **doctrines** must be the same as those of the Apostolic Church; and its leaders must be able to trace their **authority** back to the Apostles (see p. 14). Thus, history, Apostolic doctrines, and Apostolic authority are the sure guidelines for determining which Church Jesus founded. Only the Catholic Church meets these requirements.

HISTORY. Any objective history book will show that only the Catholic Church has existed since the time of Christ.[36] No Protestant denomination found today existed before 1517 A.D.

APOSTOLIC DOCTRINES. The early Church Fathers are our indispensable link to Apostolic Christianity. Their writings tell us what the first Christians believed. A careful study of the early Church Fathers shows they all taught distinctively Catholic doctrines.

APOSTOLIC AUTHORITY. The Bible and Sacred Tradition are very clear that Christ left a Church that would be governed by a hierarchy of bishops, presbyters, and deacons with the successor of St. Peter as the head. Only the Catholic Church has such a governing hierarchy that can trace its authority—in an unbroken succession—back to the Apostolic authority established by Christ Himself.

---

36 The word "Catholic" first appears in a letter of St. Ignatius of Antioch (110 A.D.) to distinguish Christ's Church from heretical groups (Jurgens, p. 25, #65). The word "Christian" also originated in Antioch (Acts 11:26). St. Ignatius' letter indicates that, by 110 A.D., the original Christian Church was already well known as the "Catholic Church."

AVAILABLE FROM SAN JUAN CATHOLIC SEMINARS

BOOKLETS

BEGINNING APOLOGETICS 1:
How to Explain & Defend the Catholic Faith

Father Frank Chacon & Jim Burnham
Gives clear, biblical answers to the most common objections Catholics get about their faith. Helps you explain your faith clearly, defend it charitably, & share it confidently. *(40 pages, $4.95)*

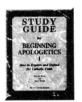

STUDY GUIDE for Beginning Apologetics 1

Jim Burnham & Steve Wood
Guides you through the handbook in 12 easy lessons. Provides discussion questions & extra material from the Bible, Catechism, & early Church Fathers. Perfect for individual or group study. *(16 pages, $3.95)*

BEGINNING APOLOGETICS 2:
How to Answer Jehovah's Witnesses & Mormons

Father Frank Chacon & Jim Burnham
Targets the major beliefs of these two aggressive groups, & shows you how to refute them using Scripture, history, & common sense. *(40 pages, $4.95)*

BEGINNING APOLOGETICS 2.5
Yes! You Should Believe in the Trinity: How to Answer Jehovah's Witnesses

Father Frank Chacon & Jim Burnham
Refutes the Jehovah's Witnesses' attack on the Trinity & provides a clear, concise theology of the Trinity.
(24 pages, $3.95)

BEGINNING APOLOGETICS 3:
How to Explain & Defend the Real Presence of Christ in the Eucharist

Father Frank Chacon & Jim Burnham
Proves the Catholic doctrine of the Real Presence from the Old & New Testament, early Church fathers, & history. Gives practical ways to increase your knowledge & love of Christ in the Eucharist. *(40 pages, $4.95)*

BEGINNING APOLOGETICS 4:
How to Answer Atheists & New Agers

Father Frank Chacon & Jim Burnham
Traces the roots of atheism & the New Age movement. Shows you how to refute their foundational beliefs using sound philosophy & common sense. *(40 pages, $4.95)*

BEGINNING APOLOGETICS 5:
How to Answer Tough Moral Questions

Father Frank Chacon & Jim Burnham
Answers contemporary questions about abortion, contraception, euthanasia, test-tube babies, cloning, & sexual ethics, using clear moral principles & the authoritative teachings of the Church. *(40 pages, $4.95)*

BEGINNING APOLOGETICS 6:
How to Explain and Defend Mary

Father Frank Chacon & Jim Burnham
Helps you answer the most common objections about Mary. Demonstrates the biblical basis for Marian beliefs & practices. *(40 pages, $4.95)*

APOLOGETICS CONCORDANCE
(or Bible Cheat Sheet)   *Jim Burnham*
Organizes over 500 verses showing the biblical basis for more than 50 Catholic doctrines—*all in two pages!* This amazing "Bible cheat sheet" helps you answer the majority of non-Catholic objections. Fold it in half, put in your Bible & never be unprepared again. *(1 sheet laminated, printed both sides, $2.95)*

BEGINNING APOLOGETICS SAMPLER

Get all 7 booklets, plus study guide and an Apologetics Concordance for a great price *($35.00; take 10% off for two or more sets. No other quantity discounts apply.)*

AUDIO TAPES

DEFENDING THE CATHOLIC FAITH
Jim Burnham
Teaches you how to charitably explain & defend your faith. Topics include: becoming an effective apologist, proving the Real Presence, appreciating the early Church fathers, & demonstrating the incorruptibility of the Catholic Church. *(Four talks on two tapes, $12.00)*

TAPES BY FATHER FRANK CHACON

Defending the Marian Dogmas (2 tapes)	**$12.00**
Proving the Real Presence (2 tapes)	**$12.00**
The Incorruptibility of the Catholic Church	**$6.00**
Reality of Devil Worship & Demonic Attack	**$6.00**
How to Respond to Homosexuality & Abortion	**$6.00**
The Great Gift of the Rosary	**$6.00**
The Death Penalty & Pope Pius XII & the Jews	**$6.00**

All prices subject to change without notice.